THE METROPOLITAN MUSEUM OF ART

CATALOGUE OF AN EXHIBITION OF EARLY CHINESE POTTERY AND SCULPTURE

BY

S. C. BOSCH REITZ

CURATOR OF THE DEPARTMENT
OF FAR EASTERN ART

NEW YORK
MCMXVI

The cost of publishing this catalogue has been largely met by private subscription among friends of the Museum whose names are withheld at their request.

LIST OF LENDERS

Smithsonian Institution
    (Charles L. Freer Collection)

Mr. Samuel T. Peters

Mr. Howard Mansfield

Mr. Albert Gallatin

Mr. James W. Barney

Mr. John Platt

Mr. Grenville Lindall Winthrop

Mr. and Mrs. Eugene Meyer, Jr.

Miss Katharine N. Rhoades

Mr. Charles W. Gould

Mr. S. K. de Forest

Mr. Alfred N. Beadleston

PREFACE

IN presenting this catalogue I must explain that I have made the most ample use of the catalogue of the exhibition held under the auspices of the Japan Society in 1914. As our object is now, as it was then, to bring before the public the best works of art and the best information available, I could not do better. The Japan Society has generously given its permission, and Mrs. Rose Sickler Williams has allowed us to reprint her exhaustive and very able report on early Chinese potteries. The identifications and descriptions then made by R. L. Hobson have been used for those numbers which were exhibited then, and new ones were made after his example. For that reason we have reproduced his Prefatory Note, which contains a great deal of valuable information. In expressing our sincere thanks for this valuable assistance, we must also mention Mr. Charles L. Freer and Mr. Samuel T. Peters, who by their substantial help and advice have done so much toward the success of this exhibition.

S. C. BOSCH REITZ.

TABLE OF CONTENTS

INTRODUCTION

IN exhibiting a loan collection of early Chinese pottery
and sculpture, The Metropolitan Museum of Art has
a double object in view: first, to encourage the interest
in Far Eastern Art by showing the best available examples;
and in the second place, by bringing together allied though
different ceramic wares, to facilitate knowledge and research.

The excellent article which was written by Mrs. Rose
Sickler Williams for the catalogue of the exhibition arranged
by the Japan Society two years ago, and which we were allowed
to reprint in this catalogue, gives the best and latest historic
and scientific information on the subject and will, no doubt,
be a great help to the student. For those who are not familiar
with the development of ceramic art in China, a few words
about the origin of, and the relation between, the different
kinds of pottery exhibited may be of use.

The exhibition was called an Exhibition of Chinese Pottery
because, although, scientifically speaking, porcelain was
made in China at a very early date, what we understand as
true porcelain was made during the Ming dynasty or little
earlier, and is not represented in our exhibition. The wares
of the T'ang and Sung periods were porcelanous earthenware or pottery. Porcelain consists of a body of kaolin
covered with a glaze of petuntse, the flesh and bone, according to Chinese authors. Kaolin is a non-fusible earth, held
together and glazed with petuntse, the same earth which,

disintegrated by millions of years, has been rendered fusible. These two substances, by nature allied, when fired together in a considerable heat form an absolutely homogeneous body which breaks or cracks but the glaze does not chip off. According to the European standard, porcelain should be translucent, resonant, and hard, that is, it cannot be scratched with a knife. The Chinese claim only resonance and hardness. As soon, however, as kaolin was used in the manufacture, the nature of porcelain was there. We know from records that this was the case in the seventh century and it may have been before. The early wares, however, retained the nature of stoneware or porcelanous pottery till the end of the Sung period, though some of the thinly potted Ting ware, as shown in our exhibition, was very translucent and several kinds were also resonant. In fact, the *Ting yao*, or Ting ware, was father to our white porcelain. It was covered with a softer, thicker, and less transparent glaze than the colorless, watery glaze of the later porcelains and therefore it is often called soft paste, a misleading and erroneous name. Soft paste or *pâte tendre* is artificial porcelain made in Europe before Boetger in 1709 found the means of making real porcelain with kaolinic earth. Real soft paste, requiring less firing and for that reason fit to be decorated with tender colors which do not stand the full heat of the kiln, was never made in China. What is called Chinese soft paste is a later product of the eighteenth and nineteenth centuries, where the porcelain earth was mixed with, or sometimes covered with, a thin coat of steatitic earth in order that a coating of thicker, more opaque glaze might be applied. The fact that the glaze was not homogeneous with the earth caused the crackle which in most cases is characteristic of this soft paste, more properly called steatitic porcelain, and which is often a charm of this dainty ware.

The earliest ware which we know in China was made in the Han period, 206 B.C.–220 A.D., earthenware covered with a green or thin yellow glaze, sometimes slightly baked without any glaze at all. The tomb figures shown in our exhibition are of this period and are chiefly chosen for their extraordinary sculptural beauty. Allied to the best Greek archaic works, they form the link between pottery and sculpture.

Chinese ceramic art developed gradually; in the T'ang period, the time when all the arts flourished in China as hardly ever afterward, the noblest forms were made, but technically, the ceramic art reached its highest point under the Sung. In Shosoin, the famous storehouse in Nara, where after the death of the Japanese Emperor Shomu, in 749 A.D., all his personal belongings and treasures were religiously kept and for the greater part are still housed, we find hard pottery covered with green and orange glazes in patches like the eighteenth-century egg-and-spinach ware, or decorated with beautiful formal patterns in blue, green, and yellow glazes on an unglazed ground. This enables us to date with certainty the similar pieces of T'ang pottery lately brought to light by the opening of early tombs in China. We show several of these pieces and among them a charming vase of pure classic lines, thinly potted and translucent, a masterpiece of the potter's art, which shows the extraordinary height of crafts-manship at this early age.

To this period, also, are ascribed certain life-size pottery figures of Lohans, of which a series has been lately brought over from China, some of which can be seen in different museums. We regret that one of these, acquired by our Museum in Berlin, owing to the present difficulties of trans-port cannot be shown. Small figures of the same class are represented and also a beautiful pair of clasped hands. Because their early date is contested by some authorities, we are glad to offer this opportunity for comparison and contro-versy, hoping thus to further the knowledge on the subject.

In the Sung period we begin to hear of different famous kilns. First and foremost, the legendary Ch'ai and Ju wares which already in the sixteenth century were said to have dis-appeared. Fortunately, a Chinese officer who accompanied an embassy to Corea in 1125, gives a description of the pottery he saw there, in which he says it resembles in color the famous Ju. For that reason we have shown some of the Corean pottery, found in tombs of the Korai period, of the very kind that the Chinese officer saw, in order to give an idea of what this beautiful, thinly potted *Ju yao* was. Some day examples of these early wares may be brought to light or discovered in existing collections; for the present, only pieces answering more or less to the old descriptions can be tentatively so ascribed. In our exhibition we do not show any of these.

The *Ting yao*, a white, creamy pottery with an exquisite soft glaze, apart from the differences of Northern and Southern Ting, *tu Ting* and *fen Ting* (for which I refer to Mrs. Williams's article), can be divided into four different classes. First, the real Ting, a hard, grayish white ware covered with a thick, soft, white glaze, plain or decorated with a moulded design. Then a grayer ware covered with a white slip before the unctuous white glaze was applied. The slip is a white earth of the nature of pipe-clay, made liquid by the addition of water, in which the raw pot is dipped after having been dried, the object being to whiten the clay where it might shine through the glaze. Then there is the crackled Ting ware, called Kiangnan ware, for convenience' sake, after R. L. Hobson, in his excellent book on Chinese Pottery and Porcelain, had suggested that such ware might have been made in Kiangnan. Fourth, I mention under the same heading the white Corean ware. One of the objects of this exhibition is, as I said before, to throw light on hitherto contested or dark points, and this is one of them.

There are those who in their great admiration of everything Chinese cannot admit the ability of other and contemporary potters. They claim therefore that the white Corean Ting ware found abundantly in Corean graves of the Korai period, that is, from before 1392, when Sungdo, the old capital of Corea, was destroyed, must have been of Chinese make imported into Corea. The letter of the Chinese officer of the year 1125, quoted before, uncomfortably contradicts their statement, because he writes: "They have, besides, bowls, platters, wine-cups and cups, flower vases and soup bowls, all closely copying the style and make of Ting ware. Only the wine-pots present novel features." The Japanese authorities also have always claimed that white Corean ware had been made, and though they say that the difference cannot be described, they still assert that to the connoisseur the difference is discernible. This difference is certainly not easy to discern and for this reason we offer comparison. Certain Corean white ware not of the finest quality has a distinct green tinge where the glaze runs thick, which seems characteristic, especially as much later and even quite late Corean ware shows the same transparent green glaze. Some more common Chinese pottery and some ware of the T'ang period exhibited here certainly show the same glaze, especially where white slip was used, and the same difficulty of differentiation exists.

Ting ware of the most beautiful kind comes extraordinarily near our standard of real porcelain, and is particularly well potted and very translucent. I want to draw particular attention in this respect to a delightful bowl, thin and graceful, of very early date, and of eggshell fineness, a masterpiece of the potter's art, and also to the seated figure of an Empress, the forerunner of the so-called *blanc de Chine* figures made at a later date in Fukien. This later Fukien or Chien ware, not to be confused with the Sung Chien ware called *Temmoku* in Japan, has followed the traditions of the *Ting yao* up to the present day. Its soft and creamy glaze reminds one of the European soft-paste porcelain. On the other hand, the very white, transparent Ting gradually developed into the real porcelain of the Ming and later periods.

Another kind of pottery, very nearly related to the *Ting yao*, is the *Tz'u-chou yao*. Its characteristic is a black or dark brown decoration in bold lines and beautiful drawing, though other decorations frequently occur through the most varied and clever use of the slip already referred to. We show different specimens where the slip has been incised in bold patterns or cut away revealing the darker ground underneath, or where the white glaze has been replaced by a dark brown or black glaze treated in the same way, incised or cut away, leaving the bare paste visible in places.

Special attention should be given to a very rare and early gray pot with an incised ornament filled in with white slip under a transparent glaze. This possibly unique jar forms the link with another well-known Corean ware, also with an incised design filled with white slip and covered with a transparent green glaze. On the origin of this particular Corean ware fortunately the authorities agree, but its Chinese prototype was up to now unknown.

Just as the black and white Tz'ŭ-chou ware was a forerunner of the later decorated porcelain, the colored Tz'ŭ-chou ware was the forerunner of the later *famille verte* and all the porcelains decorated in the muffle stove. The process of the muffle stove is the decoration with enamel colors on pottery or porcelain baked and glazed in the strong fire of the kiln. These colors could not stand great heat and were therefore refired in a much gentler heat sufficient to make them adhere to the original glaze.

Our exhibition shows a certain number of pieces decorated in green and yellow enamels and iron red, which should not be confused with the Tz'ŭ-chou pieces, decorated with red slip, which produces a duller color. Though enamel colors appear already on T'ang pottery (see No. 6), the technique is not identical, as there the colors were applied to unglazed or slightly glazed pottery and the whole piece did not require great firing, thus forming a ware more closely related to the later enamels on biscuit of the late Ming and K'ang-hsi periods.

If I may be pardoned for introducing all these technical questions and comparisons with later developments, I should like to point out here the relation to later ware of two delightful Sung pieces, one a vase with dragons in relief in different colors on a black ground, the other a finely modeled small black vase with a beautiful greenish yellow showing inside. These rare pieces of a kind difficult to class seem the fore-runners of the later pieces fired in the temperate kiln (*au petit feu*), where the colors are not applied in a second firing, but the whole piece, colors and all, is fired at once in a temperate fire.

The subject of colored glazes naturally leads us to the chief attraction of this exhibition, the *Chün yao*. We have the good fortune of being able to show a more comprehensive collection than has ever been brought together, where the rarer kind, especially the *tz'u t'ai*, or porcelanous ware, is splendidly represented. In Mrs. Williams's article it is clearly explained that the *Chün yao*, the ware made in Chün-chou during the period of Northern Sung, is divided into two very different kinds, the *tz'u t'ai* or hard paste and the *sha t'ai* or sandy paste. The fact is that these two kinds have little in common except their great beauty. A third kind, commonly called *Yüan tz'u*, of later date, is related to both, as its name implies. It has the appearance of the first, the more sandy, though darker clay of the second. In color it is generally more charming than beautiful, lacking the severe style of the earlier ware.

The fact that the first-mentioned Chün, the *tz'u t'ai*, is so perfect in workmanship has long caused these pieces to be regarded as of later date. Comparison with Ming pieces and historical evidence have, however, satisfactorily proved their extreme age. They were made for use rather than simply for decoration, and though part of them were made with tribute clay and for imperial use, in a time when taste and skill were of such high standing as under the Sung dynasty, they were outclassed by the older and much admired wares of Ch'ai, Yu, and even Northern Ting. These have un-fortunately disappeared long since, and where comparison failed the *tz'u t'ai* came to its rights. It certainly is now the rarest and most sought after of early Chinese wares. The pieces owe their delightfully varied colors to the presence of copper oxide in the glaze which, according to the heat of the kiln and the accidents of more or less air, becomes blue and purple till brilliant red comes to the surface and again disappears, and becomes green and dull in over-fired pieces. For this reason the brilliant red, the color of roses or rouge, is the most appreciated. In later times the air in the kiln was artificially regulated by drafts or by the letting in of smoke to produce the *flambé* colors, while in the early kilns the effect was so-called natural, certainly not so easily obtained, but if successful more beautiful. That in later times not only the color and the shape of the color splashes could be determined, but designs even could be produced is curiously proved by a bowl of the late Sung or Yüan period which is shown. Two Chinese letters, chun shin, meaning "purity of heart," are clearly visible and can hardly be attributed to chance. By what means, however, this was done I am not prepared to say. It is easy to trace in the existing specimens the gradual evolution of this process which ended in the loud colors of the eighteenth-century *flambés*. The great variety of effects of firing on the glaze is curiously shown by the olive-colored rims and the bases, always covered with a thin olive wash. Where the glaze ran thin at the rims and was applied thinly on the bases, the color disappeared, and left an olive-brown, except in rare patches accidentally of greater thickness, a fact which can be noted in all modern kilns where it is well known that any glaze to produce the desired color has to be applied thickly. The hard Chün invariably shows under the foot an incised number under the glaze, ranging from one to ten, sometimes with the additional letter *dai*, meaning "great." Different theories about the meaning of these numbers exist; the most likely is that they indicated the size, one standing for the largest.

The Chien ware, chiefly represented by tea bowls, known in Japan as *Temmoku*, is related to the famous hard Chün in so far as it shows in its best specimens the same streaky flecks

[xx]

of color which seem to float in the thick glaze. In this case, however, the glaze is intensely black with silvery or brown hues which have been compared to hare's fur. The clay is, however, very different, black and thick, a porous mass which has the quality of retaining the heat for a long time, for which reason the *Temmoku* bowls are much appreciated in Japan for the tea ceremony. Lately, similar bowls of much lighter clay have been found in Honan, some similar to the Chien ware, some flecked or coffee brown, some even with designs of leaves or dragons. We show several of different varieties.

A few words about the Lung-ch'üan ware or celadon remain to be said. The celadons have long been considered the earliest wares made in China. They were perhaps the earliest pieces of porcelanous ware; it is certain they were the first pieces that reached Europe. The Warham bowl treasured in Oxford in a silver-gilt mount was bequeathed in 1530, and before that dishes presented to Lorenzo de' Medici in 1487 were considered marvels; but, after all, they dated only from the end of the Yüan period or later. The fact is that the early mythical wares of Ch'ai and Ju were of the celadon type. According to Chinese description, they were the color of the sky after rain, which is a decidedly greenish blue or blue-green. They may have been extremely popular because they resembled green jade; certainly at all times Chinese potters have striven to reproduce this color, and in the eighteenth century with considerable success. The celadons known in western countries till not very long ago were mostly of moss-green hue and rarely bluish in color. They were the heavily potted types, made for export all over the world, some early, but mostly of the Yüan and early Ming periods. In Japan some rare Sung pieces of beautiful texture and light blue-green color were treasured, but only lately the early Chinese pieces have reached us, partly from tomb finds, partly from excavations made on the sites of the Lung-ch'üan kilns where wasters of beautiful color and great thinness were found. They are of light grayish white porcelanous clay covered with a very transparent blue-green glaze, though some range to warmer green and even brown. It is among these bluish hues that we must look for the early *Ch'ai* and *Ju yaos*. Our much-quoted Chinese officer who went to Corea in the Sung time compares these to the Corean celadons; for this reason we included Corean wares of this period. The great difference between these several kinds seems to have been the quality of the earth, which in some cases contained more iron and in consequence reddened in the kiln or even turned quite dark where exposed to the more or less direct heat of the fire, while in the early times it is probable also that the natural presence of iron in the glaze produced the green color.

CHINESE AND COREAN POTTERIES

ALTHOUGH for a long time past a few far-seeing and tasteful collectors have been gathering in all the chance specimens of early pottery and porcelain which have strayed from China, it is only in quite recent years that a widespread movement has been apparent in Europe and America in favour of the earlier phases of Chinese art; and nothing could be more symptomatic of this movement than the opening of an exhibition in which the Chinese section consists entirely of Sung and Yüan types.[1]

The circumstances which have made such an exclusive exhibition possible are in themselves interesting. The growing desire among Western collectors to possess examples of the beautiful Sung wares, and the consequently enhanced prices which these wares now command, have created a good market for them outside of China; and the demand has come at a time when the conditions prevailing in China, regrettable as they are from so many points of view, have set free a supply of keramic rarities which have been hitherto jealously guarded. At the same time our knowledge of the wares themselves has been greatly augmented by the finds of early pottery and porcelain in the ground which railway construction has chanced to disturb. Consequently there has been a steady stream of early wares leaving China in the last few years, potteries coarse and refined, grave-goods and collectors'

[1] This article by Mr. R. L. Hobson, printed as an introduction to the Chinese section of the catalogue of the Japan Society's exhibition of 1914, is here reprinted in exactly the same form.

[xxiii]

CHINESE AND COREAN POTTERIES

masterpieces, all of them attractive for aesthetic or antiquarian reasons. Indeed, it is surprising how few of these old
potteries, even of the roughest of them, are devoid of aesthetic
appeal; while of the true representations of the Sung pottery
words are impotent to describe the subtle beauty and charm.

They are true children of the potter's art, reflecting in their
strong but graceful contours, in the skilful finish of their simple
forms, the loving touch of a master hand. They are clothed
in the purest of keramic adornments—glaze, and in most
cases glaze alone. Sometimes decoration in relief (carved,
applied, or pressed out by moulds), or in fine, firm lines traced
with a metal point, is added, true keramic methods which
consist of adding or subtracting clay and clay. Even when
the adventitious aid of the painter's brush is requisitioned,
the pigment used is almost always a coloured clay.

But the outstanding feature of the Sung and Yüan wares
is the beautiful colour which pervades the glaze,—colour due
in part to infinitesimal quantities of iron and copper oxides
transformed by the magic of the fire into innumerable shades
of green and brown, crimson and purple, turquoise and even
black, but due perhaps more especially to opalescence, the
happy accident of an immature technique in which the thick,
slow-flowing, irregular glaze, full of minute bubbles and pin-
holes, breaks up the light as it receives it into unimagined
combinations of prismatic colours. This is the secret of the
ever-changing tints of the Chün ware, to which age has added
a further charm by investing the surface of the glaze with a
faint iridescent lustre.

Add to these the smooth soft green of the celadon and the
refined ivory and waxen whites of the Ting wares, and the
growing admiration for the early Chinese potteries needs no
further explanation. Indeed, the colours of the Sung and
Yüan glazes are the most subtle and at the same time the most
sensuous in the whole range of keramic art.

Nor is this all. Compared with later Chinese porcelains,
the early wares have the advantage of appealing more strongly

[xxiv]

to the sporting instinct at the back of every collector's mind. The former are well known and easily placed, and they can be acquired without difficulty by those who have the means. The latter are still rare enough to require hunting, and they are a difficult, elusive, and often dangerous quarry worthy of a true collector's steel. The knowledge of them has only just begun: there are new fields to be explored and fresh discoveries to be made. At present we have tasted just enough of their quality to make our appetite insatiable.

As to their classification, it is still largely tentative and must remain so until systematic excavation is made and literary evidence is supplemented by spade-work. One type of Chün ware, for instance, is clearly established; but the same name is used to cover other large groups, one of which, called "soft Chün" in the catalogue, differs widely in its buff-red paste and crystalline glaze from the traditional Chün type. One or two kinds of Ko ware are recognised, while others and the cognate Kuan wares are still conjectural and as misty as the smooth lavender-grey glaze which I have tentatively associated with the name of Kuan in the descriptions. The typical Lung-ch'üan celadon is well known, but there are many other celadons awaiting identification; and the same partial recognition has been reached in the large group of Ting wares. There is, in fact, abundant scope for research and discovery.

Literary evidence has been our mainstay hitherto, and the results, though incomplete, are not altogether negligible. A single instance will serve to illustrate its value and at the same time to introduce the Corean wares which are described in another section of the catalogue. Hsü-ching was an officer in the suite of Lu Yun-t'i, who went on an embassy to Corea in 1125, and among the notes which he made on that country are the following instructive paragraphs:

"The wares of Kao-li (Corea) which are green (*ch'ing*) in colour are described as *fei* (kingfisher) by the people of the country. In recent times the fashion of these wares has been clever, and the colour and glaze even better (than the form).

The shape of the wine pots is like a gourd, with small cover on the top in the form of a duck squatting on a lotus flower. They have, besides, bowls (*wan*), platters (*t'ieh*), wine cups (*pei*) and (tea) cups (*ou*), flower vases and soup bowls (*t'ang chan*), all closely copying the style and make of Ting ware. . . . Only the wine pots present novel features.

"In Kao-li the drinking vessels and dishes for the banquet table are mostly of gilt metal or silver, but green pottery vessels are also highly prized. There are, besides, lion (*suan i*) incense-burners which are also *fei* colour. The creature squats on top of the vessel, supported by an upturned lotus. Of all the wares, only these are of exceeding excellence. The rest have a general resemblance to the old *pi-sê* (secret colour) ware of Yüeh-chou and the recent wares of Ju-chou."

As we are quite familiar with the Corean celadon, we obtain from this last passage a clear hint as to the nature of two rare Chinese wares.

R. L. HOBSON.

LIST OF CHINESE DYNASTIES

Shang Dynasty . . . . 1767–1122 B. C.
Chou Dynasty . . . . . 1122–256 B. C.
Shin Dynasty . . . . 256–206 B. C.
Han Dynasty . . . 206 B. C.–220 A. D.
Wei Dynasty . . . . 220–265 A. D.
The Six Dynasties . . . 265–618 A. D.
T'ang Dynasty . . . . 618–906 A. D.
The Five Dynasties . . . 906–960 A. D.
Sung Dynasty . . . . 960–1280 A. D.
Yüan Dynasty . . . . 1280–1368 A. D.
Ming Dynasty . . . . 1368–1644 A. D.
Ch'ing Dynasty . . . 1644–1912 A. D.

CATALOGUE

CATALOGUE

T'ANG PERIOD

1 Vase in the shape of a pilgrim bottle with broad foot, low neck, and two handles. Decorated with a classic-looking design of two dragons; light whitish buff ware covered with a transparent, iridescent glaze, finely crackled.
T'ang dynasty.
H. 7¾ in. D. 6½ in.

2 Vase in the shape of a pilgrim bottle with broad foot, low neck, and two handles. Decorated with a classic-looking design of a phoenix between grape vines; light buff clay covered with a brown glaze mottled with greenish black.
T'ang dynasty.
H. 8⅝ in. D. 7¼ in.

3 Vase with globular body, flaring mouth, spreading foot, and two small handles. Of classical purity of design and evidently strongly influenced by early Greek art. Very fine white paste covered with a thin, transparent glaze which has almost entirely disappeared, and decorated with a raised and impressed ornament of leaves and formal branches.
T'ang dynasty.
H. 4 in. D. 4⅞ in.

4 Vase with graceful ovoid body, wide mouth with low rim, and small base. Thin and highly translucent porcelanous ware which seems almost bodiless. The glaze is of delicate pearly gray tint, crackled, and faintly clouded with minute brown specks. The base, which is only partially covered with glaze, shows a white body rough with kiln-sand.

The form of this exquisite vase is Grecian, and it is probably the earliest piece of translucent porcelain as yet published. Sung dynasty or earlier.
H. 3⅛ in.   D. 3⅛ in.

5   Vase of baluster form with high shoulders and small, spreading neck. Of buff-colored soft clay covered with brown-black glaze, finely crackled, leaving the clay to show through in a design of flowering plum branches.
Tz'ŭ-chou type: T'ang dynasty.
H. 7 in.   D. 5 in.

6   Dish on three feet. Of whitish buff paste covered with thin, finely crackled greenish glaze, decorated in the center with an incised pattern filled in with blue, green, and yellow enamels.
T'ang dynasty.
H. 2⅜ in.   D. 11¼ in.

7   Incense-burner on three feet. Hard buff paste, the upper part covered with white slip and a finely crackled, transparent glaze with splashes of blue and yellow, making a formal pattern.
T'ang dynasty.
H. 4¾ in.   D. 6¾ in.

8   Pot of globular form and short, wide lip with two handles in the shape of animals, intended to hold rings. Hard buff paste, the upper part covered with thin white slip and a thin, transparent glaze splashed with blue and green enamels. Six moulded medallions covered with green and yellow enamels have been applied around the neck and body.
T'ang dynasty.
H. 7⅜ in.   D. 7 in.

9   Vase with two handles in the shape of dragons. Light buff paste, the upper part covered with green and orange finely crackled glaze.
T'ang dynasty.
H. 13½ in.   D. 7½ in.

10   Small tomb pillow of so-called agate ware, composed of layers of yellowish white and brown clay; in places covered with the remains of a thin, transparent glaze.
T'ang dynasty.
H. 2⅛ in.   D. 4¼ in.

11 Globular pot with wide, low neck. Decorated with an incised formal pattern in four bands. The incised design has been inlaid with white slip; the neck and inside are covered with the same slip. A thin, transparent glaze covers the entire surface and ends in an irregular line near the foot. This vase is interesting as the prototype of the technique used by the Coreans in their decoration of Korai celadons.
T'ang dynasty.
H. 5 in. D. 5½ in.

12 Bulbous vase with low, spreading neck, of light, reddish buff clay covered with white slip and carved in a pattern of flowering branches; about the neck a band of conventional leaves. Covered with a thin, transparent glaze mostly deteriorated.
Tz'ŭ-chou type: T'ang dynasty.
H. 5⅛ in. D. 6 in.

13 Vase with oviform body, spreading neck, and broad foot; neck broken off. Soft white paste covered with white, orange, and green glaze in patches. Decorated with a formal design of phoenix between iris flowers and on the reverse a huntsman surrounded by the same formal design.
T'ang dynasty.
H. 9¾ in. D. 5½ in.

14 Incense-burner on five legs resting on a ring. Buff paste covered with white, green, and orange glaze in patches, egg and spinach pattern.
T'ang dynasty.
H. 4¼ in. D. 6 in.

15 Ewer with handle, in the shape of two dragons drinking and a spout in the shape of a bird's head. Hard buff paste covered with finely crackled green glaze.
T'ang dynasty.
H. 18½ in. D. 9 in.

16 Vase with pear-shaped body, long neck, and flaring, scalloped lip. Decorated with bands of flower scrolls and long leaves about the bottom and neck. The paste is light gray, burned reddish in firing; very light in weight. Transparent glaze, finely crackled, green where it has run thick.
T'ang dynasty.
H. 13½ in. D. 5 in.

17 Vase with pear-shaped body, and spreading, scalloped mouth. Light buff paste covered with white glaze over which is a yellow glaze, of which only traces remain except inside the mouth.
T'ang dynasty.
H. 12½ in.   D. 5 in.

18 Vase in the shape of a bronze with globular body, long neck, and high foot. Light buff clay reddened in the firing and covered with transparent, crackled greenish glaze.
T'ang dynasty.
H. 9¼ in.   D. 5¼ in.

19 Pear-shaped vase with slightly spreading neck decorated with a band of flower scrolls and long leaves round the bottom. Light buff ware burned red, light in weight, and covered with transparent, finely crackled glaze turned green where it has run thick. The paste has burnt red in the design, where the glaze is thin.
T'ang dynasty.
H. 9 in.   D. 5 in.

20 Small, pear-shaped vase on a high foot, with wide mouth, and a pierced design of lotus flowers, the bottom covered with lotus leaves. Light buff clay, light in weight, burned brown, and covered with minutely crackled, transparent glaze.
T'ang dynasty.
H. 4⅞ in.   D. 3 in.

21 Small, octagonal, pear-shaped vase with short neck. Light gray clay burned brown; decorated with eight panels filled with flower scrolls and covered with greenish transparent glaze.
T'ang dynasty.
H. 6¾ in.   D. 3¾ in.

22 Small bowl of conical shape with rounded sides. Hard, grayish buff ware covered with a thin, transparent glaze, crackled and water stained.
Kiangnan type: T'ang dynasty.
H. 1¾ in.   D. 4¼ in.

23 Small box of light, reddish buff clay covered with a regular design in white, orange, blue, and green glazes.
T'ang dynasty.
H. 1½ in. D. 3¼ in.

24 Small figure of a sitting Lohan of light-colored buff clay. The hands and garments are covered with yellow, green, and white glaze, finely crackled and in patches. The face and chest are left unglazed.
T'ang dynasty.
H. 6¼ in. D. 4 in.

25 Miniature vase of baluster shape with two scroll handles. Fine buff ware covered with a white slip and a green, finely crackled glaze; ornamented in brown pigment with a sketchy drawing of an iris in a flower pot, and partly covered with an orange-yellow sediment.
T'ang dynasty.
H. 4 in.

26 Miniature vase of baluster shape with two small handles moulded in the shape of masks and rings. Covered with a white slip and a yellow, finely crackled glaze; decorated with splashes of green, yellow, and red enamel suggesting a flower.
T'ang dynasty.
H. 4 in.

TING WARE

27   Globular vase with long neck decorated with two bands of raised key pattern. Finely crackled white glaze over hard porcelanous ware.
Kiangnan ware: Sung dynasty.
H. 16½ in.   D. 11½ in.

28   Vase with graceful ovoid body and small mouth. Translucent porcelanous ware with ivory-white glaze, clouded in parts with smoky brown stains.
Probably made at Ching-tê-chên: Sung dynasty.
H. 7¾ in.   D. 6¾ in.

29   Vase with slender ovoid body and high, narrow neck with flaring mouth. Hard buff-white ware with a wheel-made band on the shoulder and on the neck. Creamy glaze of uneven flow, flawed in places and stained by age.
T'u Ting ware: Sung dynasty.
H. 21 in.   D. 7½ in.

30   Pot of globular form with wide, straight, short neck; of hard buff ware covered with a creamy white glaze.
T'u Ting ware: Sung dynasty.
H. 5 in.   D. 5½ in.

31   Vase with slender, pear-shaped body and tall, tapering neck, slightly spreading at the mouth. Reddish buff stoneware with creamy glaze having fine "fish-roe" crackle, faintly tinged with brown.
Probably Sung ware of the Ting class, made in the Kiangnan factories.
H. 18¼ in.   D. 7 in.

32 Vase with graceful ovoid body, short contracted neck, and flanged mouth, the line being broken at the shoulder by a slightly raised ridge and three wheel-made bands incised. White porcelanous ware with ivory-white glaze and a few faint brownish "tear-stains": flat base beveled at the edge.
Ting, probably Ching-tê-chên ware: Sung dynasty.
H. 13 in.   D. 7½ in.

33 Sprinkler of bronze form. Ovoid body, slender neck, and flange projecting at the top, ending in a fine point. Small spout with cup-shaped mouth. White porcelanous ware with creamy glaze.
T'u Ting ware: Sung dynasty.
H. 8¾ in.   D. 4 in.

34 Vase with oval, melon-shaped body and high neck, with flaring mouth and low foot. Gray-buff ware covered with white slip and thick creamy glaze. Rim fitted with copper band.
T'u Ting ware: Sung dynasty.
H. 8¾ in.   D. 4½ in.

35 Vase with graceful ovoid body and short, narrow neck with spreading mouth. Reddish buff stoneware with a solid, smooth white glaze of ivory tone faintly browned by age. The glaze is minutely crackled and has the texture and lustre of an egg.
Ting type, probably made at Tz'ŭ-chou or in one of the Shansi factories: Sung dynasty or earlier.
H. 14⅛ in.   D. 7½ in.

36 and 37   A pair of conical bowls with small foot and straight sides, the mouth rim bare and fitted with a silver band. Hard buff-white ware with lightly moulded ornament under a warm, creamy glaze which is irregularly crackled. Inside is a lotus flower at the bottom and a design of flowering lotuses growing up the sides, edged with a band of key-fret, called "cloud and thunder" pattern by the Chinese.
T'u Ting ware: Sung dynasty.
H. 3¾ in.   D. 7¾ in.

38 Bowl of wide conical form with straight sides and small foot. Hard buff-white ware with ornament moulded in low relief under a creamy white glaze, slightly crackled on the exterior.

[9]

The mouth rim is bare and fitted with a silver band. Inside is a lotus flower at the bottom and a design of three fish among lotuses and aquatic plants on the sides, edged with a band of key-fret or "cloud and thunder" pattern.
T'u Ting ware: Yüan dynasty.
H. 3¼ in. D. 8 in.

39 Conical bowl with straight sides. Inside decorated with design of chrysanthemums and at the center the symbol *yin-yang*. Hard white ware with beautiful thin, white glaze, unintentionally crackled. The mouth rim is bare and fitted with a metal band.
T'u Ting ware: Sung dynasty.
H. 3 in. D. 7 in.

40 Bowl of conical form with small foot and gently curving sides. Hard buff-white ware with ornament strongly etched with a pointed instrument under a soft, yellowish glaze minutely crackled and clouded with a light, smoky brown stain: the mouth rim unglazed and fitted with a copper band. Inside, a lotus flower at the bottom and lotus scrolls in archaic design on the sides.
T'u Ting ware: Sung dynasty.
H. 3½ in. D. 6 in.

41 Flat dish of white-buff paste with creamy white glaze. Decorated with moulded design, a goose among flowers with border of phoenixes and chrysanthemums between a double border of "cloud and thunder" pattern. Unintentionally crackled.
Pai Ting ware: Sung dynasty.
H. 2¼ in. D. 11⅞ in.

42 Vase, bottle-shaped with depressed globular body and tall, slender neck with a ten-lobed bulb at the mouth. Dense buff stoneware with creamy crackled glaze clouded with dull reddish brown stains. Etched ornament consisting of five bats (emblems of the five blessings) among *ju-i* cloud scrolls. A border of gadroons and of key-fret at the junction of shoulder and neck, and a band of stiff plantain leaves on the neck.
The *wu fu*, or five blessings, are Riches, Happiness, Longevity, Peace and Tranquillity, and An End Crowning the Life.
T'u Ting ware: Yüan dynasty.
H. 12 in. D. 8¼ in.

43 Vase with ovoid body, short contracted neck, and spreading
mouth. Reddish brown stoneware with thick cream glaze
shading off into faint brown in places, and lightly stained here
and there with purple. Crackled glaze. The ornament is borrowed from an antique bronze, and consists of a belt of key-
fret and *k'uei* dragon pattern outlined in low relief, and a band
of round-headed studs on the shoulder.
Probably made in the province of Kiangnan: Sung dynasty.
H. 17⅜ in. D. 10¼ in.

44 Beaker-shaped vase of bronze form, white porcelanous ware
covered with yellowish, finely crackled glaze.
Kiangnan ware: Sung dynasty.
H. 18½ in. D. 6½ in.

45 Vase with broad, pear-shaped body, short neck, and wide,
spreading mouth. Reddish brown stoneware with closely
crackled cream glaze, stained by age and corrugated under the
base. The form and ornament are taken from an antique
bronze, and the latter consists of a belt of *k'uei* dragon-fret, a
border of *ju-i* heads on the neck, and a band of studs on the
lower part of the body.
Probably made in the province of Kiangnan: Sung dynasty.
H. 9¾ in. D. 10 in.

46 Vase with tall, slender body gently rounded at the shoulders,
neck cut off, and wide mouth. Buff-white stoneware with
yellowish creamy glaze closely crackled in "fish-roe" pattern
and clouded with brown stains. The surface is uneven like
orange peel.
Ting type, probably made in the province of Kiangnan: Yüan
dynasty.
H. 19½ in. D. 5¾ in.

47 Vase with slender ovoid body, short contracted neck, and
spreading mouth. Reddish brown stoneware. The glaze has a
rough granular surface, usually compared with that of an ostrich
egg. Inside the mouth the granulations are exaggerated and
the glaze has a shark-skin texture. The ornament is borrowed
from an antique bronze, and consists of a belt of key-fret and
k'uei dragon pattern outlined in low relief, and a band of
round-headed studs on the shoulder.

[11]

Probably made in the province of Kiangnan: Sung dynasty.
H. 17⅝ in.   D. 10¼ in.

48   Basin of conical form with gently curving sides and small foot.
Hard buff-white ware with ornament moulded in low relief
under a faintly crackled glaze of warm cream color. The
mouth rim is bare and fitted with a metal band. In the center
is a fish and on the sides a design of fishes among lotuses and
aquatic plants.
T'u Ting ware: Sung dynasty.
H. 3⅜ in.   D. 9¼ in.

49   Vase of slender ovoid form with short neck and small mouth.
Hard white ware with faintly crackled cream glaze which has
flowed unevenly in light brownish "tear-stains." Through the
glaze dimly appears a formal lotus scroll freely incised and
covering the whole surface.
T'u Ting ware: Sung dynasty.
H. 12½ in.   D. 5½ in.

50   Basin of conical form with gently curving sides and small foot.
Hard buff-white ware with ornament moulded in low relief
under a faintly crackled glaze of warm cream color. The
mouth rim is bare and fitted with a silver band. In the center
is a fish, and on the sides a design of three fishes among lotuses
and aquatic plants, bordered by a band of key-fret or "cloud
and thunder" pattern.
T'u Ting ware: Sung or Yüan dynasty.
H. 4⅛ in.   D. 13½ in.

51   Vase with slender ovoid body and small neck with flanged
mouth. Buff stoneware with white slip coating which reaches
almost to the base, and a colorless glaze. The surface is
minutely crackled and has the solid ivory-white appearance of
the choicest Satsuma ware.
Probably made in the province of Shansi: Sung dynasty or
earlier.
H. 9¾ in.   D. 5 in.

52   Basin of conical form with gently curving sides and small foot.
Hard buff-white ware with ornament moulded in low relief
under a faintly crackled glaze of warm cream color. The

mouth rim is bare and fitted with a silver band. Chrysanthemum flowers and leaves on the sides and "cloud and thunder" band above.
T'u Ting ware: Sung dynasty.
H. 3⅛ in.   D. 9¾ in.

53   Globular vase with tall, spreading neck and incised pattern of flowers and leaves. Gray-buff ware covered with thick yellowish glaze.
Ting ware: Sung dynasty.
H. 13½ in.   D. 6¾ in.

54   Large dish with engraved design of fishes and border of water plants. Buff-white ware with thick creamy white glaze, beautifully crackled.
Pai Ting ware: Yüan dynasty.
H. 1½ in.   D. 10⅞ in.

55   Bowl of conical form with slightly rounded sides in the shape of a six-petaled flower, decorated with peonies in moulded pattern. White porcelanous clay covered with yellowish cream glaze showing tear stains on the outside.
T'u Ting ware: Sung dynasty.
H. 2¼ in.   D. 7¼ in.

56   Quadrangular vase of bronze form with wide shoulders, contracted neck with sides almost straight, and slightly expanded mouth; low, hollow base. Hard buff-white pottery covered with white slip and a sparsely crackled glaze of uneven flow, and showing brownish passages where it has run thick. Boldly incised ornament consisting of a belt of formal lotus designs inclosed by scrolled foliage. Borders of *ju-i* scrolls at the base; of false gadroons inclosing cusped ornament on the shoulders; and of key-fret or "cloud and thunder" pattern on the neck.
Ting ware: Sung dynasty.
H. 20 in.   D. 14¼ in.   W. of a side, 10 in.

57   Flask of pilgrim bottle shape. Porcelanous ware with slip cover and ornament moulded in low relief under creamy glaze. On each side are dragons and "cloud and thunder" borders.
T'u Ting ware: Yüan dynasty.
H. 13¼ in.   D. 8½ in.

[13]

58 Vase in form of a flattened, flask-shaped bottle with short, straight, round neck and hollow, oval foot. Thin white pottery of moderate hardness, with designs moulded in low relief under a faintly crackled, yellowish glaze which has flowed unevenly here and there and formed in thick patches and drops. On one side is a three-clawed, full-face dragon among *ju-i*-shaped clouds and flame scrolls, grasping a "pearl." On the other side is a phoenix standing on one leg among *ju-i* clouds. Borders of key-fret or "cloud and thunder" pattern. The *ju-i* ("as you wish") sceptre, which has a head like the *ling-chih* fungus, is an auspicious object which brings fulfilment of wishes. Conventional cloud scrolls commonly end in a form suggesting the *ju-i* head and embodying its auspicious meaning. T'u Ting ware: Yüan dynasty.
H. 14¼ in. D. 11½ in.

59 Pilgrim bottle of flattened flask form with two dragon handles at the neck. Porcelanous ware with ornament moulded in low relief under a cream-white glaze. On each side are scrolls of conventional peonies (the *fu kuei* flower, symbolizing riches and honors) with *ju-i*-shaped petals in their centers, inclosing bats, which are emblems of happiness: borders of key-fret or "cloud and thunder" pattern.
T'u Ting ware: Yüan dynasty.
H. 12 in. D. 8¾ in.

60 Bowl with straight flaring sides curving inward toward the foot. Porcelanous white ware with creamy greenish white glaze. Decorated with flowers in six compartments and border of "cloud and thunder" pattern.
Pai Ting ware: Yüan dynasty.
H. 2½ in. D. 5⅞ in.

61 Bowl of conical form with slightly rounded sides. White porcelanous ware covered with thin white glaze unintentionally crackled. Decorated with carved lotus flowers.
Pai Ting type: Yüan dynasty.
H. 2¼ in. D. 7⅛ in.

62 Bowl of conical form with small foot. Gray porcelanous earth covered with a thick, creamy white glaze. Carved ornament of lotus flowers.
T'u Ting ware: Sung dynasty.
H. 2 in. D. 8 in.

63 and 64　A pair of vases of pilgrim bottle shape with moulded
　　pattern of dragons.　Gray porcelanous ware with thick
　　crackled glaze.
　　Fên Ting ware: Sung dynasty.
　　H. 8½ in.　D. 6 in.

65　Flat, deep dish with straight border decorated with a moulded
　　design of a lion playing with a ball, and floral border.　White
　　porcelanous ware turned red in firing.　Covered with yellow
　　glaze.
　　T'u Ting type, made at Ching-tê-Chên: Yüan dynasty.
　　H. 2⅜ in.　D. 9⅛ in.

66　Bowl of conical form with small foot and six-foil mouth rim.
　　Slightly translucent porcelain with ivory-white glaze and faint
　　brownish "tear-stains."　Boldly carved ornament consisting of
　　a lotus flower in the bottom and a lotus scroll on the side within
　　and without.　Metal band on rim.
　　T'u Ting ware: Sung dynasty.
　　H. 8¼ in.　D. 3⅛ in.

67　Saucer dish with fluted sides and narrow rim with wavy edge.
　　Porcelanous ware with ivory-white glaze: moulded design on
　　the interior.　The unglazed edge is fitted with a copper band.
　　In the center is a Buddhistic figure holding over his head a bowl
　　of lotuses surrounded by a halo of flames; beside him is a deer,
　　the Taoist symbol of longevity, and in the spaces are two bowls
　　of growing lotus plants.　On the sides are floral sprays repeated
　　in each of the flutes, and on the rim is a pattern of overlapping
　　leaves.
　　Pai Ting ware: Yüan dynasty.
　　D. 8¼ in.

68　Dish with narrow, flat rim.　Porcelanous ware with ivory-white
　　glaze: the edge bare and fitted with a silver band.　In the
　　center is a beautiful scroll of formalized lotus or peony flowers
　　with feathery foliage boldly carved; on the rim is a running
　　foliage scroll etched with a point.
　　T'u Ting ware: Sung dynasty.
　　D. 10 in.

69　Saucer dish with six-lobed edge.　Porcelanous ware with
　　moulded design in low relief under an ivory-white glaze: "tear-
　　stains" on the outside.　The mouth rim is unglazed and fitted

with a copper band. Inside is a peony scroll with three semi-nude boys among the branches.
Pai Ting ware: Sung or Yüan dynasty.
D. 7¾ in.

70 Cup and cover in the shape of a lotus flower. Buff porcelanous ware covered with white glaze.
T'u Ting ware: Sung dynasty.
H. 3½ in.   D. 3 in.

71 Cup with rounded sides on tall foot. White porcelanous earth with thin glaze beautifully crackled.
Kiangnan ware: Sung dynasty.
H. 2⅞ in.   D. 5⅝ in.

72 Six-lobed bowl of white porcelanous earth covered with white glaze, green where it has run thick; transparent.
Pai Ting type: Sung dynasty.
H. 2¾ in.   D. 5 in.

73 Cup-stand of ovoid body on saucer with a high foot. Fine porcelanous earth covered with a thin creamy glaze, tear drops under the saucer.
Pai Ting ware: Sung dynasty.
H. 3⅜ in.   D. 4½ in.

74 Small bowl of conical form with straight sides. Buff-white ware with ornament of archaic lotus flowers moulded in relief beneath a finely crackled yellow glaze. Copper band over the mouth rim.
T'u Ting ware: Sung dynasty.
H. 1¼ in.   D. 4 in.

75 Small bowl with rounded sides. Yellowish white stoneware covered with white slip and a transparent glaze, leaving a ring at the bottom of the cup uncovered.
Ting ware: Yüan dynasty.
H. 1⅜ in.   D. 3¾ in.

76 Cup in form of six-petaled flower. Translucent fine white ware covered with creamy white glaze.
Pai Ting type: Sung dynasty.
H. 1⅜ in.   D. 4½ in.

[16]

77　Small bowl with rounded sides, moulded in form of lotus flower. White porcelanous ware covered with grayish white glaze. Mouth rim fitted with copper band.
Pai Ting ware: Sung dynasty.
H. 1½ in.　D. 3⅝ in.

78　Basin with wide mouth, gently curving sides, and flat base. Ivory-white glaze; "tear-marks" on the exterior. The unglazed mouth rim is fitted with a silver band. Ornamented with boldly carved lotus scrolls inside and out.
T'u Ting ware: Sung dynasty.
H. 4½ in.　D. 9¾ in.

79　Seated figure of white-buff ware covered with yellow glaze.
Ting ware: Yüan dynasty.
H. 14 in.　D. 9½ in.

80　Basin with wide mouth and gently curving sides. Covered with ivory-white glaze; unglazed mouth rim fitted with copper band. Inside ornamented with boldly carved lotus scrolls.
T'u Ting ware: Sung dynasty.
H. 4½ in.　D. 10¼ in.

81–82　Two dishes, small, flat, six-lobed; white porcelanous ware, thinly potted, transparent, and covered with unctuous transparent glaze; fired upside down, rims unglazed.
Ting ware: Sung dynasty.
H. ½ in.　D. 3½ in.

83　Ladle, the rim covered with copper. Covered with creamy white glaze.
T'u Ting type: probably Sung dynasty.
L. 4¾ in.

84　Small vase of globular form with long, straight neck, flaring lip, and high foot. On the body are two dancing figures which serve as handles; white porcelanous ware covered with a thick unctuous glaze.
Ting ware: attributed to Sung dynasty.
H. 6 in.　D. 3 in.

[17]

85 Small pilgrim bottle of buff-colored stoneware covered with white slip and thick yellowish glaze. Moulded pattern of phoenix.
Fên Ting ware: Sung dynasty.
H. 4½ in.   D. 5¼ in.

86 Seated figure of Kuan Yin, in her diadem a small figure of Buddha on a lotus. Fine white porcelanous paste covered with a transparent crackled glaze.
Sung dynasty.
H. 9½ in.   W. 4¾ in.

TZ'Ŭ-CHOU WARE

87 Baluster-shaped vase with small neck. Hard buff ware covered with white slip and green transparent glaze.
Tz'ŭ-chou type: Sung dynasty.
H. 15¾ in. D. 7½ in.

88 Jar with ovoid body, short neck, and low, cup-shaped mouth. Hard buff ware decorated with flowers in white slip under a cover of green, finely crackled glaze partly gone and leaving a thin, transparent coating. The earth where it is not covered with slip shines through gray. Beautiful iridescent spots where the glaze has deteriorated.
Tz'ŭ-chou type: T'ang dynasty.
H. 15⅞ in. D. 8¾ in.

89 Vase of slender baluster form with tall, narrow neck and wide, saucer-shaped mouth with flat sides. Grayish white porcelanous ware with white slip which stops in an uneven line above the base, and a smooth grayish white glaze; graffito ornament showing white against a mouse-gray ground. On the body is a bold floral scroll with etched details, and on the shoulder is a foliage scroll. There is a band of wheel-made lines in the middle of the neck.
Tz'ŭ-chou ware: Sung dynasty.
H. 20 in. D. 7¼ in.

90 Pear-shaped vase with spreading neck. Buff stoneware covered with white slip and thin, transparent glaze. The slip is cut away in three bands of phoenix and cloud design and ornamental leaves.
Tz'ŭ-chou ware: Sung dynasty.
H. 12⅜ in. D. 7 in.

91 Slender, pear-shaped vase: hard gray porcelanous ware covered
with white slip and transparent glaze, the slip partly etched
away to leave a large floral design on a gray background.
Tz'ŭ-chou ware: Sung dynasty.
H. 14 in.   D. 6 in.

92 Pear-shaped bottle: reddish buff stoneware covered with slip
which is etched away to form the decoration; a floral design
arranged in two broad bands, and one narrow horizontal band;
at the base a design of formal leaves.
Tz'ŭ-chou ware: Sung dynasty.
H. 12¼ in.   D. 7 in.

93 Vase of slender oval form with small neck and conical mouth.
Gray stoneware coated with white slip over which is a colorless
glaze minutely crackled.   Graffito ornament in three broad
bands.   In the central band is a bold foliage scroll with the
background cut away and etched details showing white against
a mouse-colored ground: below this is a formal pattern of
vandykes and arches with slashed lines between; and on the
shoulder is a foliage scroll with etched outlines and details,
the background powdered with small, impressed circles.
Tz'ŭ-chou ware: Sung dynasty.
H. 18½ in.   D. 8 in.

94 Vase of slender oval form with small mouth.   Buff stoneware
with a coating of solid white slip and a creamy white glaze,
boldly painted with belts of ornament in black.   On the sides
is a broad band of floral scroll; below it a narrower band with
three foliage sprays, which is repeated on the shoulder: stiff
leaves round the foot.   The glaze is shrunk in shallow wrinkles
on the upper part.
Tz'ŭ-chou ware: Sung dynasty.
H. 16⅝ in.   D. 7½ in.

95 Vase, slender with narrow, short neck; hard gray porcelanous
stoneware covered with white slip and thin, transparent glaze;
slip etched away, leaving a broad band of floral ornament, with
a narrower band below; at the base formal leaves.
Tz'ŭ-chou ware: Sung dynasty.
H. 18 in.   D. 7½ in.

96 Vase with pear-shaped body, high broad shoulders, short contracted neck, and wide mouth. Reddish stoneware. The design executed in graffito etching through a wash of thin black, the incisions disclosing the white slip beneath. The figures in the panels in this case represent three sages—one looking at a lotus in a pool, another pointing to a skeleton on the ground, and the third standing before a blossoming tree: in each panel are rocks and bamboos and clouds floating above. The belts of ornament are separated by white bands painted with concentric rings in black.
Tz'ŭ-chou ware: Yüan dynasty.
H. 12⅞ in.   D. 11⅜ in.

97 Pillow. Hard gray stoneware covered with white slip and transparent glaze. Decorated in brownish black with the figures of a sage and a stork; on the front and ends are floral designs. Impressed mark on bottom.
Tz'ŭ-chou ware: Sung dynasty.
H. 5½ in.   L. 12 in.

98 Pillow in the shape of a tiger. Hard gray stoneware covered with thick white glaze and decorated in black.
Tz'ŭ-chou ware: Sung dynasty.
H. 4¼ in.   L. 10¼ in.

99 Vase of slender ovoid form with short neck and flattened lip. Buff stoneware covered with white slip which has been etched away and filled in with purplish black to form a floral scroll in two horizontal bands. The background is covered with small circles. At the base is an incised design of tall leaves.
Tz'ŭ-chou ware: Sung dynasty.
H. 16½ in.   D. 7½ in.

100 Vase of pear shape. Hard gray stoneware covered with white slip and a transparent thin glaze decorated with iron-red, green enamel, and gray-black. The main design is a broad band containing three pointed quatrefoils, two containing figures and boats, the third a formal floral design; on the shoulder is floral ornament and around the base a design of formal floral leaves; the inside is enameled black.
Tz'ŭ-chou ware: Sung dynasty.
H. 12½ in.   D. 13 in.

101 Vase of slender oval form with small mouth. The neck is cut off. Buff stoneware with a coating of solid white slip and transparent crackled glaze, boldly painted in red with scenes representing two figures making offerings to a figure on a lotus throne. Stiff leaves around the foot. On the shoulder is a formal foliage scroll. The background covered with small circles.
Tz'ŭ-chou ware: Sung dynasty.
H. 15½ in. D. 7¾ in.

102 Dish of dark buff ware covered with white slip and transparent, finely crackled glaze. Decorated with flowers in iron-red, green, and yellow enamels.
Tz'ŭ-chou ware: Sung dynasty.
H. 1⅝ in. D. 6¾ in.

103 Dish; circular, flat, with upturned rim. Grayish white stoneware, covered with a white, finely crackled glaze and decorated with the phoenix amid flowers and leaves outlined in iron-red on a background of green enamel and surrounded by green and yellow enamel bands.
Tz'ŭ-chou ware: Sung dynasty.
H. ¾ in. D. 8 in.

104 Bowl, deep and cylindrical. Gray stoneware covered with slip and a transparent glaze and decorated with iron-red, green, and yellow enamels.
Tz'ŭ-chou ware: Sung dynasty.
H. 3¼ in. D. 4½ in.

105 Bowl of conical shape and slightly rounded sides. Of buff stoneware with double slip cover and transparent glaze and decorated with flowers in iron-red and green enamel.
Tz'ŭ-chou ware: Sung dynasty.
H. 2¼ in. D. 6⅝ in.

106 Vase with pear-shaped body, high broad shoulders, short contracted neck, and wide mouth: a wide flange at the base. Reddish stoneware with wash of white slip and transparent glaze. Painted ornament in black with touches of orange slip under the glaze. The main design is a broad band con-

taining three pointed quatrefoil panels with figure subjects: (1) a garden terrace with a seated personage and an attendant giving him wine; (2) a similar figure reclining in a garden under a fruit-laden tree; and (3) an interior with a man sleeping. The spaces are filled with scrollwork. On the shoulder is a broad belt of foliage scrolls with four large flowers at even intervals; and there are narrow borders of key-fret, vandyke, and scroll patterns, and a band of false gadroons on the foot. The base is edged with a broad black band.
Tz'ŭ-chou ware: Yüan dynasty.
H. 13½ in. D. 11¼ in.

107 Bulbous vase with long, spreading neck of gray stoneware covered with white slip and yellowish finely crackled glaze. Inside the neck is covered with green glaze.
Tz'ŭ-chou type: Sung dynasty.
H. 19 in. D. 10 in.

108 Vase with pear-shaped body, high broad shoulders, short contracted neck, and wide mouth; a wide flange at the base. Reddish stoneware covered with white slip; painted ornament in brown with touches of orange slip. The main design is a broad band with three pointed quatrefoil panels, two of which contain each a stork; the band on the shoulder contains floral ornament; around the base is a band of false gadroons.
Tz'ŭ-chou ware: Sung dynasty.
H. 13½ in. D. 12 in.

109 Figure of Kuan Yin. Hard porcelanous stoneware, decorated with white and red slip and outlined with black under a transparent glaze.
Tz'ŭ-chou ware: Yüan dynasty.
H. 11¾ in.

110 Vase, slender, with small neck and four handles. Dark buff stoneware covered with white slip over reddish slip under a thin, transparent glaze; the lower half is covered with dark brown glaze; on the upper half are Chinese characters in brown.
Tz'ŭ-chou ware: Sung dynasty.
H. 10 in. D. 4¾ in.

111 Vase of reddish buff clay covered with white slip and colorless transparent glaze. Decorated with a conventional flower design of gray-green under the glaze and an inscription in an upright panel at one side. Lip and foot cut off.
Tz'ŭ-chou ware: Sung dynasty.
H. 5¾ in. D. 4¾ in.

112 Vase of conical shape with short, round neck and sloping lip. Light yellowish stoneware covered with white slip and thin, transparent glaze. The slip is cut away in four bands of floral decoration, the background being formed by the glazed earth of the vase.
Tz'ŭ-chou ware.
H. 11¼ in. D. 4½ in.

CHÜN WARE

113 Deep bowl of globular form slightly contracted at the mouth; small foot. Gray porcelanous ware with beautiful opalescent glaze of pale lavender-blue sown with faint greenish points and ending in a billowy roll at the base. Glaze under the foot and an unglazed patch inside.
Chün ware: Sung dynasty.
H. 6⅛ in.   D. 7½ in.

114 Deep bowl of globular form slightly contracted at the mouth; small foot. Gray porcelanous ware with opalescent glaze of pale lavender-blue ending in billowy line at the base. Glaze under the foot and an unglazed patch inside.
Chün ware: Sung dynasty.
H. 5¾ in.   D. 7¾ in.

115 Bowl of conical form with small foot and contracted mouth. Buff porcelanous ware with pitted opalescent glaze of greenish gray faintly streaked; where the glaze has run thick at the rim, olive-gray shows. The foot is washed with thin olive-gray glaze and has a patch of the general gray glaze.
Chün ware: Sung dynasty.
H. 3⅛ in.   D. 5¾ in.

116 Bowl of conical shape with rounded sides. Hard, reddish buff ware covered with a finely speckled and crackled greenish blue, opalescent glaze, brown where the glaze has run thin.
Chün ware: Sung dynasty.
H. 3½ in.   D. 5¾ in.

117 Bowl of globular form, slightly contracted at the mouth; small foot. Gray porcelanous ware burnt red-brown at the foot and on the mouth rim, which are both bare. Smooth

opalescent glaze of exquisite moon-white color passing into pale lavender. A patch of glaze under the foot.
Kuan ware: Sung dynasty.
H. 4⅛ in.   D. 6⅛ in.

118   Bowl of conical form with small foot and slightly contracted mouth. Porcelanous ware burnt reddish brown at the base. Thick opalescent glaze heavily bubbled on the upper parts and irregularly crackled, the color deep lavender-gray with light brown flecks here and there and a flush of purple on the upper part of the exterior. A patch of glaze under the base.
Chün ware: Sung dynasty.
H. 3⅜ in.   D. 6 in.

119   Flower pot with globular bowl, high neck, flaring mouth, and low foot slightly spreading. Gray porcelanous ware with smooth opalescent glaze freely crackled and parted here and there with "earthworm" markings. The color is lavender finely flecked with gray and deepening into purple on the bowl: the edges are olive. The base is washed with olive-brown, incised with the numeral i, − (one), and pierced with five holes.
Chün ware: Sung dynasty.
H. 10⅛ in.   D. 10½ in.   D. of base, 6⅛ in.

120   Bulb bowl of bronze form with three cloud-scroll feet: the exterior is bordered by two rows of studs, the upper row inclosed by raised bands. Grayish white porcelanous ware with opalescent glaze irregularly crackled. An olive tint appears on the salient parts where the glaze is thin, but over the rest of the surface the color is a misty lavender-gray, more opaque and gray inside, but slightly suffused with purple on the exterior. The base is washed with olive-brown and incised with the numeral san, 三 (three), and it has a ring of spur-marks.
Chün ware: Sung dynasty.
H. 3⅟₁₆ in.   D. 9 in.

121   Bulb bowl, or flower-pot stand, moulded in six shaped lobes and flanged at the mouth with a six-foil rim: three cloud-scroll feet. Gray porcelanous ware with opalescent glaze which flows away from the salient parts, leaving them a pale gray-

olive color. The inside is blue-lavender dappled with grayish white and broken by numerous "earthworm" markings. The color outside is the same, showing slight touches of purple. The base is washed with reddish olive-brown and incised with the numeral *wu*, 五 (five); and it has a ring of slight spur-marks.
Chün ware: Sung dynasty.
H. 2⅝ in.   D. 8⅝ in.

122   Bulb bowl of bronze form with three cloud-scroll feet: bordered on the exterior with two rows of studs, the upper row inclosed by raised bands. Grayish white porcelanous ware with finely mottled opalescent glaze of misty gray color clouded with lavender and pale olive-green: the latter color appears where the glaze has run thin on the salient parts. The base is washed with olive-brown and incised with the numeral *i*, — (one), and it has a ring of spur-marks.
Chün ware: Sung dynasty.
H. 3¾ in.   D. 10½ in.

123   Bulb bowl, or flower-pot stand, moulded in six shaped lobes with flanged rim in six-foil form and three cloud-scroll feet. Gray porcelanous ware with opalescent glaze. The salient parts where the glaze is thin are a pale olive color. The inside is a bluish lavender dappled with greenish white and broken by very numerous "earthworm" markings. The color outside is the same, broken by the rounded contours of the moulding. The base is washed with olive-brown with a few red splashes and incised with the numeral *i*, — (one).
Chün ware: Sung dynasty.
H. 3⅛ in.   D. 9½ in.

124   Beaker-shaped vase of bronze form with cylindrical body, spreading foot, and high, spreading neck ornamented with vertical ribs, the remains of the bronze prototype. Gray porcelanous ware covered with greenish white, finely crackled glaze much pitted by air bubbles; the paste shows a buff color where the glaze has run thin. The foot is covered with a thin wash of bluish glaze.
Chün ware: Sung dynasty.
H. 8¼ in.   D. 6½ in.

125 Flower pot of oblong, hexagonal form with straight sides gently tapering toward the base, which is supported by six small cloud-scroll feet: narrow, flat flange at the mouth. Grayish white porcelanous ware with finely striated opalescent glaze of pale purplish color, heavily streaked with opaque milky gray on the upright surfaces and dappled with the same color on the flat parts. "Earthworm" markings on the bottom inside, and seven holes in the base. The salient parts, where the glaze is thin, are of a pale olive color. The base has brown glaze overrun with lavender and gray, and a ring of spur-marks; and the numeral *ssŭ*, ꝏ (four), is incised inside one of the feet.
Chün ware: Sung dynasty.
H. 6 in.   L. 10⅛ in.   B. 6¾ in.

126 Flower pot of deep bowl form moulded in six shaped lobes and flanged at the mouth with a six-foil rim. Grayish white porcelanous ware with opalescent gray glaze shot with faint violet and shading off into pale olive at the edges of the mouldings. The base is washed with olive-brown and incised with the numeral *wu*, Ⅴ (five).
Chün ware: Sung dynasty.
H. 6⅝ in.   D. 9½ in.

127 Part of beaker-shaped vase of bronze type; of gray porcelanous ware covered with opalescent light blue-green glaze, frothy on the neck, beautifully transparent and streaked with green-gray on the body. The paste where the glaze has run thin shows a light olive color.
Chün ware: Sung dynasty.
H. 4½ in.   D. 5 in.

128 Flower-pot stand of oblong, rectangular form with notched corners, straight sides, flanged rim, and four small cloud-scroll feet. Grayish white porcelanous ware with opalescent glaze irregularly crackled and parted with "earthworm" markings. The color is a misty lavender-gray with passages of milky white, passing into pale olive where the glaze has run thin. The base is washed with olive-brown and incised with the numeral *shih*, + (ten), and it has a ring of spur-marks.
Chün ware: Sung dynasty.
H. 2 in.   L. 7 in.

[28]

129 Bowl of conical form with small foot and slightly contracted mouth. Gray porcelanous ware burnt rusty red on the base rim. Smooth opalescent glaze faintly crackled and of pale lavender-gray color. Glaze under the base.
Chün or Kuan ware: Sung dynasty.
H. 4¼ in. D. 8¾ in.

130 Bowl with small foot and slightly contracted mouth. Grayish white porcelanous ware with smooth opalescent glaze of dove-gray color faintly tinged with lavender. Glaze under the base.
Chün or Kuan ware: Sung dynasty.
H. 3½ in. D. 8¾ in.

131 Bowl of conical form, with rounded sides and slightly contracted rim of gray-white porcelanous ware covered with light blue-gray opalescent glaze mottled and streaked with greenish white. At the rim where the glaze runs thin the paste shows through olive-gray. The foot is washed with reddish olive glaze and has a patch of blue glaze in the center.
Chün ware: Sung dynasty.
H. 4 in. D. 9 in.

132 Dish with narrow, flanged rim. Gray porcelanous ware covered entirely with a crackled opalescent glaze of pale lavender tint, frosted over in places with a brownish film broken here and there by "earthworm" marks. Five spur-marks under the base.
Chün ware: Sung dynasty.
D. 7½ in.

133 Plate of grayish white porcelanous ware covered with a bluish green opalescent crackled glaze; where the glaze runs thin at the rim the paste shows through pinkish gray. The foot rim is washed with reddish olive glaze and the base is covered with the general glaze. Three spur-marks.
Chün ware: Sung dynasty.
H. 1⅛ in. D. 7 in.

134 Vase of baluster form, shaped in four lobes; high shoulders and small neck. Reddish buff ware with thick opalescent turquoise glaze lightly crackled and much deteriorated; on the shoulders two bright purple splashes.
Soft Chün type: Yüan dynasty.
H. 8 in. D. 4 in.

135   Vase of baluster form, shaped in four lobes: high shoulders
and small mouth.   Reddish buff ware with thick opalescent
turquoise glaze lightly crackled and almost entirely trans-
muted into dull purple, which is broken here and there by
"earthworm" markings.
Soft Chün type: probably Sung dynasty.
H. 6⅛ in.   D. 3 in.

136   Bowl of globular form, with straight sides and slightly contracted at the mouth.   Reddish buff stoneware covered with a
thick turquoise crackled glaze on the inside, and on the outside a rich purple glaze fading into light brown where at the
rim the glaze runs thin.   The inside of the foot is covered with
a finely crackled turquoise glaze.
Soft Chün ware: Sung dynasty.
H. 2¼ in.   D. 3¾ in.

137   Small, twelve-lobed bulb bowl resting on six cloud-scroll feet.
Gray porcelanous ware glazed inside with a turquoise-blue
finely crackled and partly deteriorated glaze.   The flat border
and the exterior are covered in mottled purple, and the base
is covered with turquoise-blue and incised with the numeral
san, 三 (three).
Soft Chün ware: Yüan dynasty.
H. 2 in.   D. 7 in.

138   Small vase of bulbous shape with wide, spreading mouth and
three knobs on the neck, of buff porcelanous earth burned
reddish and covered with greenish white regularly crackled
glaze which has slight crimson splashes.   Base inside covered
with the same finely crackled glaze.
Soft Chün ware: Sung dynasty.
H. 2¾ in.   D. 2½ in.

139   Vase with depressed globular body, short neck, and projecting
lip, decorated with finely moulded lotus flowers and tall
leaves round the neck.   Buff hard stoneware covered with a
rich but thin brown-black glaze, the design showing in
brown lines where the glaze has run thin on the sharp edges
of the mouldings.   The inside is covered with a beautiful
greenish yellow glaze finely crackled and the inside of the foot
rim shows the same glaze, but coarser and greener.
Chün type: probably Sung ware.
H. 3⅜ in.   D. 2¾ in.

[30]

140   Vase with globular body, and short neck expanding into a wide, flat flange at the mouth. Reddish buff ware with thick opalescent glaze faintly crackled, the color dull turquoise with passages of lavender and shading off into dull purplish tone on the sides. The glaze on the mouth rim is deeply flawed by the bursting of bubbles.
Soft Chün type: probably Sung ware.
H. 9⅝ in.   D. 10¾ in.

141   Water pot, melon-shaped with five lobes; small mouth, short spout, and loop handle with a bud-shaped thumb-piece. Reddish buff ware with thick opalescent turquoise glaze, lightly crackled and breaking into crimson on the lower parts.
Soft Chün type: probably Sung dynasty.
H. 3⅛ in.   D., with spout and handle, 3¼ in.

142   Cup on high stem of buff stoneware burned reddish brown and covered inside with a gray-green glaze with two crimson blotches. The outside is evenly covered with crimson grading off to green-gray and ending in a billowy line near the base. The foot inside is uncovered.
Soft Chün ware: Sung dynasty.
H. 2¾ in.   D. 3¾ in.

143   Water dropper in form of a squatting hen with one chicken on its back and the head of another appearing from under its wing: cleverly modeled. Soft reddish buff ware with opaque crackled glaze of white color faintly tinged with turquoise, broken here and there by small splashes of dark ruby-red. The glaze is much decayed, and incrusted with a brownish film, and shows an occasional iridescence. There is an oval opening in the back, and the beak is pierced to serve as a spout.
Soft Chün type: Sung dynasty.
H. 6 in.   L. 6¼ in.

144   Vase with globular body and short, narrow neck slightly tapering upward. Buff ware with thick opalescent turquoise glaze lightly crackled.
Soft Chün type: Sung dynasty.
H. 4 in.   D. 3½ in.

[31]

145 Vase of ovoid shape with long, spreading neck, the foot pierced in five places. Reddish porcelanous ware covered with a finely crackled blue glaze mottled with purple, which covers the base and fills up two of the perforations in the foot.
Soft Chün ware: Sung dynasty.
H. 4½ in. D. 2¼ in.

146 Vase of baluster form, shaped in four lobes: high shoulders and small neck. Reddish buff ware with thick opalescent turquoise glaze lightly crackled and shading off into faint purple on one side. Two curious pointed oval depressions appear on the other side, caused by the bursting of air bubbles.
Soft Chün type: probably Sung dynasty.
H. 8¼ in. D. 4¾ in.

147 Vase of globular form, the exterior moulded like a lotus flower with raised petals. Dark gray stoneware burnt reddish brown on the base and the inside, which are both unglazed. Closely crackled, milky gray glaze, which is darkened on the salient parts by the body-color beneath it. The base shows the impression of a circular support.
Sung dynasty.
H. 7 in. D. 9⅛ in.

148 Vase with pear-shaped body, the lower part moulded with slightly raised lotus petals: contracted neck and spreading mouth with raised studs suggesting the seed-pod of the lotus. Buff stoneware with thick opalescent glaze minutely crackled, and of turquoise color passing into lavender and sky blue and fading into a dull purple on the sides.
Soft Chün type: probably Sung dynasty.
H. 14¼ in. D. 8¼ in.

149 Baluster-shaped vase with short neck of light buff stoneware covered with opalescent gray-green glaze streaked with blue and splashed with purple and crimson.
Chün ware: Yüan dynasty.
H. 12½ in. D. 6¾ in.

150 Incense vase with three feet, globular body, short, straight neck with flanged mouth, and two upright, rectangular handles with attachments of dragon form. Dark gray stoneware burnt

brown in the unglazed parts, with thick flowing glaze, faintly crackled, which ends in a billowy line without entirely covering the base and the feet. Applied relief ornaments overrun by the glaze, but apparently consisting of two tiger-masks on the sides and four rosettes on the neck. The glaze is opalescent and of pale lavender or *clair-de-lune* color shot with grayish white and flushing in parts with a warm purplish tinge.
Chün type: Sung or Yüan dynasty.
H. 8½ in.   D. 7½ in.

151   Vase with pear-shaped body and tall, spreading neck. Lower part moulded with raised lotus petals. Buff stoneware with opalescent glaze, minutely crackled and of turquoise color passing into reddish brown where the glaze has run thin.
Soft Chün type: probably Yüan dynasty.
H. 7¼ in.   D. 3¾ in.

152   Vase with pear-shaped body, the lower part moulded with slightly raised lotus petals: contracted neck and spreading mouth with raised studs, suggesting the seed-pod of the lotus. Buff stoneware with opalescent glaze minutely crackled, and of turquoise color passing into lavender and sky blue and fading into a purplish brown.
Soft Chün type: probably Sung dynasty.
H. 6 in.   D. 4¼ in.

153   Incense-burner with globular body, straight neck, and flanged mouth. Light buff porcelanous ware with thick crackled glaze of turquoise-green and dark purple, ending in a billowy line, the bottom and legs covered thinly with the purple glaze.
Soft Chün ware: Sung dynasty.
H. 4 in.   D. 4¾ in.

154   Vase of baluster form with high shoulder and small mouth. Reddish buff ware with crackled turquoise glaze faintly tinged with lavender, and frosted with brown on the sides.
Soft Chün type: probably Sung dynasty.
H. 6⅜ in.   D. 3½ in.

155   Vase of lotus-bud shape with a very small opening at the top. Reddish buff ware with thick opalescent glaze of turquoise color faintly crackled and frosted in places with pinkish brown.
Soft Chün type: probably Sung dynasty.
H. 2½ in.   D. 2½ in.

156   Vase with conical, bud-shaped body and small mouth. Reddish buff ware with thick opalescent turquoise glaze, lightly crackled and shading off into faint purple.
Soft Chün type: probably Sung dynasty.
H. 3⅛ in.   D. 3 in.

157   Plate with narrow, flat rim with six-foil edge. Gray-white porcelanous ware with opalescent glaze of pale lavender-blue, faintly crackled with irregular lines. Hollow base partially glazed.
Chün ware: Sung dynasty.
D. 7⅝ in.

158   Vase of oval form with small low neck and projecting lip. Buff pottery burnt reddish at the base rim, with thick opalescent glaze finely crackled and ending just short of the foot outside. The color is turquoise-blue warming into lavender, with large flushes of rosy purple.
Soft Chün type: Sung or Yüan dynasty.
H. 9 in.   D. 5⅝ in.

159   Vase of ovoid form with small mouth. Reddish buff ware with thick opalescent turquoise-blue glaze crackled and forming in billowy lumps on the sides and splashed with three symmetrical crimson patches on the shoulder.
Soft Chün type: probably Sung dynasty.
H. 4½ in.   D. 2¾ in.

160   Vase, melon-shaped with eight shallow lobes: low neck and base. Buff pottery with opalescent turquoise-blue glaze finely crackled and flowing unevenly so that the body-color shows through in places. Light tinges of purple and crimson and greenish patches appear here and there.
Soft Chün type: Sung dynasty.
H. 4¾ in.   D. 6 in.

[34]

161 Vase of pomegranate form with S-shaped foot. Reddish buff ware with thick opalescent glaze of turquoise color faintly crackled, and frosted in places with brown and splashed with crimson.
Soft Chün type: probably Sung dynasty.
H. 3 in.   D. 2⅝ in.

162 Small pear-shaped vase, with short, spreading neck; of reddish buff stoneware covered with a very thick crackled blue glaze mottled with white and covered with a purple splash.
Soft Chün ware: probably Sung dynasty.
H. 5 in.   D. 3¼ in.

163 Basin with small foot and rounded sides slightly contracting at the mouth. Buff stoneware with thick opalescent crackled glaze ending in a billowy roll just short of the base. The color inside is turquoise tinged with lavender and broken by three symmetrically placed splashes of purple dappled with crimson and in one case shading off into green. Outside it passes from purple streaked with gray into lavender with a passage of turquoise-gray and dapplings of crimson.
Chün type: Sung or Yüan dynasty.
H. 3¼ in.   D. 8⅝ in.

164 Basin with small foot, rounded sides, and slightly contracted mouth. Reddish buff stoneware with thick opalescent glaze, faintly crackled and ending in a fairly even line short of the base. The color inside is opal-blue passing into lavender-gray and heavily bubbled where it has flowed thick in the bottom of the bowl; it is broken by three splashes on the sides and one in the center, of purple with passages of crimson, frosted with green and russet brown in the centers. Outside it changes from crimson to purple shot with gray, dappled and frosted with green. An exquisite specimen with wonderful play of color.
Chün type: Sung or Yüan dynasty.
H. 4 in.   D. 9¼ in.

165 Vase with pear-shaped body and long, spreading neck; of buff-colored porcelanous ware covered with a crackled gray-blue glaze and splashed with purple. Much stained by moisture. The bottom of the foot has been covered with blue glaze.
Chün ware: Sung dynasty.
H. 1¼ in.   D. 5 in.

166 Bowl of conical shape with rounded sides and broad, heavy foot, of reddish buff clay covered with an opalescent blue glaze ending in a billowy line and drops above the foot and streaked with purplish blue lines turning to brown at the rim.
Chün ware: Sung dynasty.
H. 3¼ in.   D. 7¼ in.

167 Bowl of conical form with small foot and slightly contracted mouth. Buff stoneware with thick opalescent glaze ending in an irregular welt above the base. The color of the glaze is pale lavender-gray, or *clair-de-lune*, flecked with brown in places and broken by large patches of purple filled in with gray and greenish brown.
Chün type: Sung or Yüan dynasty.
H. 3⅝ in.   D. 6 in.

168 Bowl of conical form with small foot and slightly contracted mouth. Iron-gray stoneware with thick fluescent glaze which runs into a deep pool inside and ends in a billowy roll and large drops short of the base outside. The color changes with the flow of the glaze, from a thin brownish skin at the edge through a dark peacock-blue to light blue streaked with purple. The pool inside has boiled up into brownish gray scum and burst in large bubbles like lava.
Chün type: Yüan dynasty.
H. 3 in.   D. 7 in.

169 Bowl of conical form, with small foot and slightly contracted mouth. Reddish stoneware with thick, flowing glaze which runs into a deep pool inside and ends in a billowy roll and large drops short of the base on the outside. The color changes with the flow of glaze, from a thin brown skin at the edge through a bluish lavender to a greenish gray streaked with blue. The pool inside has boiled up into a yellowish white scum and burst in large bubbles.
Chün type: Yüan dynasty.
H. 3 in.   D. 7½ in.

170 Jar with broad ovoid body, short neck, and wide mouth. Buff stoneware with crackled opalescent glaze of pale lavender, assuming an olive tint where the glaze is thin. Three sym-

metrically disposed patches on the shoulder of green color shot with blue run into creamy white.
Chün type: Yüan dynasty.
H. 11¼ in.   D. 12¼ in.

171   Jar with broad ovoid body, short neck, and wide mouth. Dense reddish stoneware with lightly crackled opalescent glaze of pale misty lavender color assuming an olive tint where the glaze is thin: faint "earthworm" markings here and there, and three symmetrically disposed patches on the shoulder of purple color with frosted green centers. Glaze under the base.
Chün type: Sung dynasty.
H. 10⅜ in.   D. 13 in.

172   Vase with broad ovoid body, short neck, and wide mouth. Coarse reddish stoneware with crackled opalescent glaze ending in an uneven line short of the base. The color is grayish lavender of varying depth, lightly frosted in parts with brown and broken on the shoulder by three large splashes of purple with crimson centers.
Chün type: Yüan dynasty.
H. 6¼ in.   D. 7½ in.

173   Saucer dish with scalloped sides, and a large peach-blossom with leaves modeled in low relief inside. Porcelanous stoneware burnt reddish brown on the raw base. Thick opalescent glaze with wonderful play of color and freely crackled. The color passes from pale transparent greenish brown on the salient parts to lavender-blue finely flecked with gray; there are occasional spots and streaks of deep crimson-brown, and two patches of amethystine purple with dark brown centers frosted with green. A greenish gray froth partially obscures the lavender ground. The same glaze appears outside, but with large areas of transparent green.
Chün ware: Sung dynasty.
D. 8½ in.

174   Bowl of conical form with small foot and slightly contracted mouth. Coarse reddish stoneware with thick opaque crackled glaze which ends in an uneven line short of the base. The color is a pale smoky gray with a faint tinge of lavender, and

there is a splash of crimson inside frosted over with green. The glaze has shrunk into deep corrugations on the lower part of the exterior.
Chün type: Yüan dynasty.
H. 3⅜ in.   D. 7¼ in.

175   Bowl of conical form with small foot and contracted mouth. Iron-gray stoneware with opalescent glaze sparsely crackled and ending short of the base.   The color is moonlight white or very pale lavender faintly frosted with brown and broken by two purple patches with pale centers.
Chün type: Yüan dynasty.
H. 3 in.   D. 7⅛ in.

176   Bowl of conical form with small foot and slightly contracted mouth.   Gray porcelanous ware burnt brown at the foot. Opalescent glaze strongly crackled and stopping at the foot in an uneven line.   The color is milky lavender shading into pale olive at the edges and broken by two splashes of amethystine purple.
Chün type: Sung or Yüan dynasty.
H. 2¾ in.   D. 7 in.

177   Bowl of conical form with small foot and slightly contracted mouth.   Iron-gray stoneware with flowing opalescent glaze which is boldly crackled and ends in an uneven welt just short of the base.   The color is purplish lavender shot with milky gray which dominates the purple where the glaze flows thick.   Portions of the surface are thickly flecked with brown and there is a purple splash inside with a brown center.
Chün type: Yüan dynasty.
H. 3¼ in.   D. 7 in.

178   Bowl of conical form with small foot and slightly contracted mouth.   Buff stoneware with thick opalescent glaze lightly crackled and stopping short of the base.   The color is lavender-gray clouded with brown and broken by a long narrow splash of rose-purple frosted in the center with green and brown. The glaze outside is waxen in surface and deeply pitted.
Chün type: Yüan dynasty.
H. 4¼ in.   D. 8⅞ in.

179 Basin with small foot, rounded sides, and contracted mouth. Reddish buff stoneware with crackled opalescent glaze flowing in waves on the exterior and ending in an uneven roll short of the base. The color inside is lavender with purple splashes, one of which has a green-streaked center and russet spots. Outside it is milky lavender lightly clouded with a greenish brown frosting.
Chün type: Sung or Yüan dynasty.
H. 3⅞ in. D. 8⅞ in.

180–181 Two globular pots, each with wide contracted mouth and two small handles; reddish buff stoneware covered with thick, flowing, greenish white, opalescent glaze, streaked with lavender and splashed with purple and crimson, which ends in a billowy roll and large drops at the base.
Chün ware: Yüan dynasty.
H. 4¼ in. D. 5½ in.

182 Saucer dish of dark buff stoneware with opalescent glaze, crackled. Color greenish lavender-gray splashed with crimson bordered with purplish gray.
Chün type: Sung dynasty.
D. 8½ in.

183 Saucer dish of reddish buff stoneware and opalescent glaze. The color is greenish gray with regularly placed splashes of crimson and purple with brownish green centers.
Chün type: Sung dynasty.
D. 8½ in.

184 Baluster-shaped vase with short neck of hard brown stoneware covered with a thin opalescent lavender glaze turned olive-brown where the glaze has run thin, and ending a half inch above the base in a billowy line. The foot is covered with a thin reddish olive wash, and the base with bluish glaze.
Chün ware: Sung dynasty.
H. 14 in. D. 6½ in.

185 Vase with broad, pear-shaped body, high shoulders, and small, straight neck. Reddish buff porcelanous stoneware with thick opalescent glaze widely crackled and ending in a ragged line and big drops about three inches short of the

foot: below this is a thin skin of translucent glaze of olive-green color clouded with lavender-gray at the bottom. The main glaze is covered with a skin of green frosting which has parted in a netting of "earthworm" marks and spots revealing a gray color beneath, with tinges of purple which emerge in a warm flush on one side.
Chün type: Sung or Yüan dynasty.
H. 10 in.   D. 7¼ in.

186   Incense-burner with globular body, straight neck and flanged mouth, two dragon handles, and three small feet. Gray porcelanous ware with opalescent and faintly crackled glaze passing from gray to lavender and splashed with large patches of purple.   An unglazed patch inside.
Chün ware: Sung dynasty.
H. 3⅜ in.   D., with handles, 5⅛ in.

187   Incense-burner with globular body, straight neck, and flanged mouth.   Gray porcelanous ware with faintly crackled opalescent glaze of pale lavender-blue with splashes of purple which shade off into crimson and violet.   Unglazed inside the bowl.
Chün ware: Sung dynasty.
H. 8⅜ in.   D. 4¼ in.

188   Incense-burner with globular body, straight neck, and flanged mouth.   Dark buff porcelanous body with faintly crackled greenish white glaze with a faint purple splash, and glazed base.
Soft Chün ware: Yüan dynasty.
H. 2⅜ in.   D. 2⅝ in.

189   Saucer dish with narrow flanged rim. Porcelanous ware burnt red at the base, which is unglazed: the rest of the surface covered with a smooth opalescent glaze of pale delicate lavender-gray or *clair-de-lune* with two patches of purple finely powdered with gray specks.   The glaze is boldly but irregularly crackled.
Probably Kuan ware: Sung dynasty.
D. 7⅛ in.

190 Plate with narrow rim. Gray porcelanous ware with opalescent glaze of misty lavender-gray color breaking into large patches of plum-purple with crimson tinges. The surface is lightly frosted with brown. Three spur-marks beneath.
Chün or Kuan ware: Sung dynasty.
D. 7⅛ in.

191 Small, pear-shaped pot with wide mouth of reddish buff stoneware covered with thick opalescent gray-green glaze splashed with purple turning to green in regular designs forming two Chinese characters, *chun shin*, meaning "purity of heart." The interest of this piece is that it clearly proves that in the later periods colored splashes on *Chün yao* could be exactly controlled.
Chün ware: Yüan dynasty.
H. 4¼ in. D. 4¾ in.

192 Water pot of depressed globular form with small mouth. Reddish buff ware with crackled opalescent glaze of turquoise color with broad band of plum-purple blotched with turquoise and faint green stains.
Soft Chün type: Sung dynasty.
H. 1⅝ in. D. 3 in.

193 Incense-burner with depressed globular body, straight neck, and flanged mouth: three small feet. Gray porcelanous ware with misty lavender-gray glaze passing into purple flecked with russet and green spots. Metal mount and cover, the latter with pierced floral design, made in Japan.
Chün ware: Sung dynasty.
H. 2⅛ in. D. 2¾ in.

194 Incense-burner with globular body, straight neck, and flanged mouth. Gray porcelanous ware with faintly crackled opalescent glaze of pale greenish gray with splashes of light purple. Part of the bowl inside unglazed.
Soft Chün ware: Sung dynasty.
H. 2⅝ in. D. 3¼ in.

195 Vase with globular body, short neck with spreading lip, and two loop-handles. Buff stoneware with thick opalescent glaze strongly crackled and ending in a fairly regular welt short

of the base. The color is pale lavender-blue flushing with purple on the sides and broken by large rose-purple splashes, with crimson flecked with gray in their centers. The shoulders are lightly frosted with brown, and the underlying purple emerges in the lines of the crackle and in the bubbles of the glaze.
Chün type: Sung or Yüan dynasty.
H. 5 in.   D. 5⅝ in.

196   Jar of oval form with contracted neck and wide mouth with thick, rounded lip. Coarse gray stoneware full of quartzlike particles, with a thick opalescent lavender-gray crackled glaze spotted with purple and madder-brown and broken by two splashes of blood-crimson, changing into deep crab-shell green, and frosted on the shoulders with brownish gray. The base and part of the interior are unglazed.
Chün type: Sung or Yüan dynasty.
H. 4¾ in.   D. 5½ in.

197   Shallow bowl of gray stoneware burnt rusty red on the foot rim. Crackled, opalescent glaze of misty gray-white tinged with lavender: splashes of purple and crimson with green and russet in their centers. Glaze inside the base.
Chün type: Sung dynasty.
H. 1¾ in.   D. 6⅝ in.

198   Saucer dish of reddish buff stoneware and opalescent glaze, sparsely crackled. The color is a misty lavender-gray faintly frosted with brown and splashed with crimson. The base has a smear of brown glaze; and the numeral *êrh*, ⼆ (two), has been incised, apparently after firing.
Chün type: Sung or Yüan dynasty.
D. 7½ in.

199   Saucer dish of pale buff stoneware with crackled opalescent glaze ending in an uneven line beside the foot rim. The color is lavender of varying depth faintly shot with gray, and on one side there is a large greenish splash shading into brown at the edge.
Chün type: Sung dynasty.
D. 9⅛ in.

200 Saucer of reddish buff porcelanous ware covered with a crackled blue-green opalescent glaze, olive-brown where the glaze has run thin and with a splash bordered with brilliant crimson.
Chün ware: Yüan dynasty.
H. 1 in.   D. 5 in.

201 Small plate of dark buff ware covered with a blue glaze clouded with brownish white and splashed with purple. Where the glaze has run thin the buff paste shows through.
Chün ware: Yüan dynasty.
H. 1¼ in.   D. 4¾ in.

202 Plate with straight sides and narrow rim. Grayish buff stoneware with crackled opalescent glaze of pale lavender-gray sown with purple points and broken by two purple splashes with green frosting in the centers: the base unglazed.
Chün type: Yüan dynasty.
D. 5¾ in.

203 Bowl of conical form with small foot and contracted mouth. Gray porcelanous ware with smooth opalescent glaze ending in an uneven line short of the base. The color inside is lavender-gray with pale olive tinges on the rim and in the parts where the glaze has run thin, small patches of purple and rusty brown, and large irregular crackle. On the outside the green and lavender pass at once into a deep purple which suffuses the rest of the surface.
Chün ware: Sung dynasty.
H. 3⅛ in.   D. 5½ in.

204 Bowl of conical form with small foot and slightly contracted mouth. Porcelanous ware burnt rusty brown in the unglazed parts. Smooth, finely crackled glaze of pale lavender-gray clouded with smoky brown and broken by purplish patches which have the bloom of a ripe peach. The base is partially glazed.
Probably Kuan ware: Sung dynasty.
H. 3 in.   D. 5½ in.

205 Globular vase with contracted mouth of yellowish buff stoneware covered with a bluish gray opalescent glaze finely crack-

led and splashed with beautiful crimson. At the mouth, where the glaze runs thin, the paste shows through a pale olive. The foot is slightly washed with transparent glaze and splashed with the general glaze.
Chün ware: Sung dynasty.
H. 3½ in.   D. 4¼ in.

206   Incense-burner of globular form, with spreading lip and three small feet. Buff porcelanous ware covered inside with a pale opalescent milky green glaze streaked with white. The outside is crimson red streaked with lavender turning into rose color and becoming pale turquoise-white on the base. The paste shows reddish olive where the glaze has run thin. The base shows five spur-marks and slight accidental crackle.
Chün ware: Sung dynasty.
H. 4⅛ in.   D. 6⅞ in.

207   Bowl of conical form with small foot and contracted mouth. Gray porcelanous ware with opalescent and evenly crackled glaze. The color inside is greenish gray; outside the same color flushed with rose-red on one side with a slightly purplish border. The foot is covered with thin olive-brown glaze and a splash of the predominating gray-green glaze.
Chün ware: Sung dynasty.
H. 3⅜ in.   D. 5¾ in.

208   Bowl of conical form with small foot and contracted mouth. Gray porcelanous ware with pitted opalescent glaze ending in an uneven line short of the base. The color inside is turquoise-green with crimson and lavender splashes, the centers of which have burned olive-green. The outside has also purple splashes with crimson edges and olive-green centers on a light turquoise-white opalescent ground. The foot is covered with a light buff glaze and has a splash of opalescent light turquoise glaze over it.
Chün ware: Sung dynasty.
H. 3⅜ in.   D. 5¾ in.

209-213   Set of five bowl-shaped cups with small feet and slightly contracted mouth rims. Porcelanous ware burnt reddish brown on the unglazed base. Smooth opalescent glaze thin

at the edge and of pale olive tint which passes into gray-dappled lavender with isolated patches and large areas of deep purple, which is in one case slightly frosted with greenish brown.
Chün ware: Sung dynasty.
H. 1⅝ in.   D. 3⅜ in.

214 Small, fluted vase, with pear-shaped body and spreading neck. Yellowish buff porcelanous ware covered with an opalescent lavender glaze streaked with blue. The paste shows through a yellowish brown where the glaze runs thin. Foot glazed inside.
Chün ware: Yüan dynasty.
H. 4 in.   D. 2 in.

215 Octagonal vase, pear-shaped, with slender neck and spreading mouth, covered with a thick black glaze, on a small octagonal stand of turquoise-blue and decorated with five dragons crawling up against the vase, each covered with a different glaze, turquoise-blue, dark indigo-blue, yellow, white, and red mottled with green, faintly crackled. The base is covered with turquoise-blue glaze and incised with the number *san*, 三 (three). The clay is sandy and grayish white.
Soft Chün type: Sung dynasty.
H. 8⅞ in.   D. 3½ in.

216 Bottle of oviform shape with short, straight neck and wide mouth; of coarse dark gray stoneware browned in firing and covered with a dark blackish brown glaze mottled and streaked with blue turning through green to yellowish white.
Chien or Chün type: Sung dynasty.
H. 17½ in.   D. 9 in.

217 Flower pot of deep bowl form. Grayish white porcelanous ware with finely striated, deep opalescent glaze of greenish blue color covered with brilliant purple. Inside is a dark greenish blue color of deep tone. The rim where the glaze has run thin is olive color. The base perforated by five holes is washed with olive-colored thin glaze and incised with the numeral *ssŭ*, 四 (four).
Chün ware: Sung dynasty.
H. 8 in.   D. 10 in.

218 Flower pot, companion to the above, and of the same shape. The finely striated deep opalescent grayish blue glaze of lighter color than No. 217 is more evenly covered with vivid dark rose in fine lines. The opalescent grayish blue interior shot with faint violet is also lighter in color. The rim and the base where the glaze is thin are olive color. The base pierced with five holes bears incised the numeral *ssŭ*, ⊕ (four).
Chün ware: Sung dynasty.
H. 8 in.   D. 10 in.

219 Flower pot with globular body, short neck, and low, spreading foot: five holes in the bottom. Grayish white porcelanous ware, burnt rusty red on the unglazed edge. Opalescent glaze of singular beauty with minute crackle, and a belt of "earthworm" marks on the neck. The color changes from pure blue-opal inside the neck through warm gray to purplish lavender shot with grayish white in the interior. On the outside the gray-flecked lavender warms into rose-purple with a silken iridescent bloom on one side; and on the other side it is strongly dappled with crimson-brown specks which concentrate in a deep brownish crimson patch. The base is washed with olive-brown and incised with the numeral *êrh*, ⸗ (two).
Chün ware: Sung dynasty.
H. 6¼ in.   D. 10 in.

220 Vase of ovoid form. Grayish white porcelanous ware with finely striated glaze of dark blue color heavily streaked with light blue and rich purple, in parts turning into deep red. The inside is brilliant blue streaked with turquoise-blue and dappled with red on the bottom. The lip where the glaze is thin is of olive color. The flat base shows traces of thin brown glaze. The center is ground down in order to efface the Imperial Chinese Palace mark and the numeral *pa*, 八 (eight), which a Chinaman who knew the vase in the Imperial Collection reported was once there.
Chün ware: Sung dynasty.
H. 6⅝ in.   D. 6 in.

221 Flower pot of quatrefoil shape with flat rim; gray porcelanous earth covered inside with a blue-green opalescent glaze overflowed at the top with purple, which flows down from the

rim; where the glaze has run thin, olive-brown shows through. Outside it is evenly covered with a mottled purple glaze full of "earthworm" tracks. The base is washed with greenish olive-brown, perforated with five holes, and marked with the number *chiu*, 九 (nine).
Chün ware: Sung dynasty.
H. 4½ in. D. 8⅛ in.

222 Bulb bowl, or flower-pot stand, moulded in six shaped lobes and flanged at the mouth with a six-foil rim: three cloud-scroll feet. Gray porcelanous ware with opalescent glaze which flows away from the salient parts, leaving them a pale olive color. The inside is a purplish lavender dappled with grayish white and broken by a few "earthworm" markings. The color outside is broken by the rounded contours of the moulding and changes repeatedly from pale olive through dappled lavender to deep crimson. The base is washed with olive-brown and incised with the numeral *êrh*, 二 (two), and it has a ring of spur-marks.
Chün ware: Sung dynasty.
H. 3 in. D. 9⅜ in.

223 Bulb bowl with moulded five-foil sides, flanged mouth with rolled edges, and three cloud-scroll feet. Gray porcelanous ware with thick crackled opalescent glaze having great play of color. Inside, it is translucent olive-green clouded and mottled with gray and purple and passing into crimson on the rim, which is frosted with crab-shell green on the edges. Outside, it is mostly rose-purple dappled with lavender and gray and deepening into crimson and purplish brown. There is a light frosting in places. The base is washed with olive-brown and incised with the numeral *liu*, 六 (six), and it has a ring of spur-marks.
Chün ware: Sung dynasty.
H. 2⅝ in. D. 8¾ in.

224 Bulb bowl with sides moulded in five petal-shaped lobes, flanged rim of five-foil form with rolled edge, and three cloud-scroll feet. Gray porcelanous ware with thick opalescent glaze, with a cluster of "earthworm" markings in the center

of the interior. The color passes from light olive at the edges to plum-colored purple dappled and curded with greenish gray. The same colors appear on the outside, but the red tints are stronger and the gray, which runs down in milky waves, is deeply tinged with purple, and here and there the color deepens into brownish crimson. The base is washed with olive-brown and incised with the numeral *liu*, ☆ (six), and it has a ring of small spur-marks.
Chün ware: Sung dynasty.
H. 2⅝ in.   D. 8¾ in.

225 Bulb bowl or flower-pot stand, moulded in six shaped lobes and flanged at the mouth with a six-foil rim: three cloud-scroll feet. Gray porcelanous ware with opalescent glaze, which flows away from the salient parts, leaving them a pale olive color. The inside is a purplish lavender dappled with grayish white. The color outside is broken by the rounded contours of the moulding and changes repeatedly from pale olive to dappled lavender and deep crimson. The base is washed with olive-brown. It has a ring of spur-marks and is incised with the numeral *chiu*, ☆ (nine).
Chün ware: Sung dynasty.
H. 2¼ in.   D. 7½ in.

226 Bulb bowl, or flower-pot stand, moulded in six shaped lobes and flanged at the mouth with a six-foil rim: three cloud-scroll feet. Gray porcelanous ware with opalescent glaze, which flows away from the salient parts, leaving them a pale olive color. The inside is a greenish lavender dappled with greenish white and a few splashes of purple. The rim is purple dappled with grayish white. The color outside is slightly broken by the rounded contours of the moulding and is dark crimson mottled with lavender turning in parts to greenish gray. The base is washed with greenish olive-brown and is incised with the numeral *san*, Ξ (three).
Chün ware: Sung dynasty.
H. 2⅞ in.   D. 9¼ in.

227 Bulb bowl of bronze form with three cloud-scroll feet: the exterior is bordered by two rows of studs, the upper row inclosed by raised bands. Grayish white porcelanous ware with opalescent glaze faintly crackled. The salient points where

the glaze is thin are pale olive. Inside, the color is lavender-blue mottled and clouded with opaque grayish and greenish white broken by "earthworm" marks. On the exterior, the glaze is faintly iridescent and has a beautiful silken sheen, and the color is rose-purple finely flecked and shot with grayish white. On the feet it develops a deep crimson. The base is washed with olive-brown and incised with the numeral *ssŭ*, ⚏ (four), and it has a ring of spur-marks.
Chün ware: Sung dynasty.
H. 3¼ in.   D. 8⅝ in.

228   Bulb bowl of bronze shape with three cloud-scroll feet: bordered on the exterior with two rows of studs, the upper row inclosed by raised bands. Gray porcelanous ware with opalescent glaze, which flows away from the salient parts, leaving them a pale olive color. Inside, the glaze is purplish lavender flecked and clouded with grayish white and parted here and there with "earthworm" markings. On the outside, it changes from gray to dappled purple, developing a deep crimson on the lower part of the feet. The base is washed with dull brown and incised with the numeral *pa*, λ (eight), and it has a ring of spur-marks.
Chün ware: Sung dynasty.
H. 2¹¹⁄₁₆ in.   D. 6⅞ in.

229   Bulb bowl of bronze form with three cloud-scroll feet: the exterior is bordered by two rows of studs, the upper row inclosed by raised bands. Grayish white porcelanous ware with opalescent glaze faintly crackled. The salient parts where the glaze is thin are pale olive. Inside, the color changes from pale blue to a bluish violet flecked with white, surrounded by a greenish white ring with "earthworm" marks. On the outside it passes from purple to a faint rose-red line and on the upper ring a faint purple turns to grayish white. The base is washed with olive-brown partly turning into dull red and incised with the numeral *wu*, Ⴆ (five), and it has a ring of small spur-marks.
Chün ware: Sung dynasty.
H. 2⅞ in.   D. 7⅜ in.

230   Bulb bowl of bronze form with three cloud-scroll feet: the exterior is bordered by two rows of studs, the upper row in-

closed by raised bands. Gray porcelanous ware: opalescent glaze with mingled tints of transparent olive, gray, blue, and crimson, streaked and dappled, broken by "earthworm" markings, and faintly crackled. The glaze inside is chiefly purple, mottled and streaked with bluish and greenish gray. On the outside there is greater play of color, with wide areas of olive, faintly frosted with iridescent bubbles. The base is washed with olive-brown, incised with the numeral *i*, ‒ (one), and it has a ring of spur-marks.
Chün ware: Sung dynasty.
H. 3¾ in.   D. 10⅛ in.

231   Bulb bowl of bronze form with three cloud-scroll feet; the exterior is bordered by two rows of studs, the upper row inclosed by raised bands. Gray porcelanous ware with opalescent glaze, with mingled tints of blue-purple and crimson, faintly crackled. The glaze inside is blue turning to green on the bottom and evenly crackled. The base is washed with olive-brown, incised with the numeral *i*, ‒ (one), and it has a ring of spur-marks.
Chün ware: Sung dynasty.
H. 3⅞ in.   D. 10 in.

232   Bulb bowl of bronze form with three cloud-scroll feet: the exterior is bordered by two rows of studs, the upper row inclosed by raised bands. Grayish white porcelanous ware with opalescent glaze faintly crackled. The salient parts, where the glaze is thin, are pale olive. Inside, the color changes from a pale lavender-blue flecked with white to a greenish white with "earthworm" marks and dappling of pale lavender. On the outside it passes from greenish gray to purple mottled and flecked with grayish white and scored with "earthworm" marks of many forms. On the feet it passes from pale olive to deep crimson flecked with coral-red. The base is washed with olive-brown and incised with the numeral *i*, ‒ (one), and it has a ring of spur-marks.
Chün ware: Sung dynasty.
H. 3½ in.   D. 9½ in.

233   Bulb bowl, or flower-pot stand, with sides moulded in six petal-shaped lobes: flanged rim of wavy six-foil form rolled at the edge. Gray porcelanous ware with opalescent glaze

parted with "earthworm" markings. The color incised is dull olive frosted over with opaque gray-green, the "earthworm" marks and a number of small spots disclosing a beautiful sky blue which lies below. The outside is dappled crimson flecked with a thin green frosting and breaking at the edges into greenish gray and lavender. The feet are olive-green passing into crimson. Dull green glaze under the base, with the numeral *êrh*, 二 (two), incised, and a ring of spur-marks. Chün ware: Sung dynasty.
H. 3⅛ in. D. 9⅛ in.

234 Flower-pot stand of oblong, rectangular form with notched corners, straight sides, flanged rim, and four small cloud-scroll feet. Grayish white porcelanous ware with glaze of lavender tint more or less obscured by a gray-white froth. On the rim and exterior it passes into purple dappled and clouded with grayish white and developing passages of crimson on the feet. The base is washed with olive-brown and incised with the numeral *shih*, 十 (ten), and it has a ring of spur-marks.
Chün ware: Sung dynasty.
H. 2 in. L. 7⅛ in.

235 Vase with circular body and long, straight neck ending in a spreading mouth contracted at the lip. The neck is decorated with a heavy ring and two handles in the form of *ju-i* sceptres. The body is ornamented with two lions' heads meant to hold rings and an incised band of "cloud and thunder" pattern. Dark buff clay covered with finely crackled green glaze slightly iridescent and mottled with dashes of brownish purple.
Sung dynasty.
H. 8 in. D. 6 in.

236 Bowl of conical form with small foot and spreading mouth. Dark red ware burnt black. Thick purplish black glaze, which stops in an even welt above the base, richly dappled with large, lustrous silvery flecks.
Chien ware: Sung dynasty.
H. 3⅛ in. D. 7½ in.

237-239 Three bowls of conical form slightly compressed at the mouth: with small foot. Dark red ware burnt black.

Thick purplish black glaze, which stops short of the base, finely streaked with lustrous golden brown or silver: in one case the brown predominates on the upper part. Silver bands on the mouth rims.

These are the "hare's-fur" or "partridge" cups used in the tea contests and much prized in Japan, where they are named *temmoku*.

Chien ware: Sung dynasty.

H. 2¾ and 2½ in.   D. 5¾, 5, and 4¾ in.

240   Bowl of conical form slightly compressed at the mouth: with small foot. Dark reddish ware burnt black. Thick purplish black glaze ending in a thick roll above the base, and finely streaked with lustrous golden brown, the brown dominating the black on the upper part. Gold band on the mouth rim.
Chien ware: Sung dynasty.
H. 2⅞ in.   D. 4⅞ in.

241   Bowl of conical form with slightly compressed mouth and small foot. Dark reddish ware burnt black, with thick black glaze ending in a thick roll above the base and finely streaked with silvery purple lines. The lip covered with a silver band.
Chien ware: Sung dynasty.
H. 2⅝ in.   D. 4¾ in.

242   Conical bowl with rounded sides and small foot, of dark brown porous clay covered with an iridescent black glaze streaked with silvery bluish green turning to brown at the rim, which is covered with a metal band.
Chien ware: Sung dynasty.
H. 3 in.   D. 5⅛ in.

243   Bowl of conical form slightly compressed at the mouth: with small foot. Dark reddish ware burnt black, with thick purplish black glaze, which stops short of the base, frosted over with a purplish gray. Gold band on the mouth rim.
Chien ware: Sung dynasty.
H. 2⅝ in.   D. 4½ in.

244   Bowl of conical form with small foot and slightly compressed mouth. Dark red ware burnt black. Thick mouse-gray

glaze which stops short of the base, crackled and finely mottled with brown and gray.
Chien ware: Sung dynasty.
H. 2½ in.   D. 5⅛ in.

245   Bowl of conical form with rounded sides and slightly compressed mouth. Buff-colored clay covered with a black glaze splashed with reddish brown. The foot is unglazed.
Probably Northern China: Sung dynasty.
H. 2¼ in.   D. 5¼ in.

246   Bowl of conical form with straight sides and small foot. Porcelanous gray ware with thick purplish black glaze, dappled with large, irregular drops of golden brown frosted with green.
Chien type: Sung dynasty or earlier.
H. 2 in.   D. 5¾ in.

247   Bowl of conical form with slightly compressed mouth and small foot. Light buff paste covered with reddish brown glaze streaked with blue-green, ending in a billowy line near the rim and leaving the greater part of the base uncovered. Lip covered with a silver band. The foot unglazed.
Probably Northern China: Sung dynasty.
H. 2¼ in.   D. 5½ in.

248   Bowl of conical form slightly compressed at the mouth: with small foot. Buff ware burnt brownish red; covered with coffee-brown glaze faintly streaked with blue-green and ending in a blue pool at the bottom of the cup.
Northern China: Sung dynasty.
H. 2⅜ in.   D. 5 in.

249   Bowl of conical form with straight sides and small foot. Porcelanous gray ware having thick purplish black glaze with a few flecks of golden brown. Inside is a design of a skeleton leaf expressed in frothy golden brown and green. Metal band on mouth rim.
Chien type: Sung dynasty or earlier.
H. 2⅛ in.   D. 6 in.

250   Bowl of conical form, slightly compressed at the mouth: with small foot. Grayish stoneware burnt brown. Thick purplish

black glaze streaked and dappled with golden brown in which are a number of plum blossom reserves. Gold band on the mouth rim.
Chien type, probably Northern China: Sung dynasty.
H. 2¼ in.   D. 4⅝ in.

251   Bowl of conical form slightly compressed at the mouth: with small foot. Buff stoneware with thick black glaze mottled outside with large irregular flecks of dull green. The inside is thickly freckled with dull green in which are reserved two phoenixes (*fêng huang*) and three flowers.
Chien type, Northern China: probably Sung dynasty.
H. 2⅜ in.   D. 4⅝ in.

252   Bowl of shallow, wide-mouthed form. Gray porcelanous ware burnt reddish brown at the base, which is unglazed. Olive-green celadon glaze frosted and stained with brown and interrupted inside the bowl by a broad ring which is almost bare of glaze. Inside, a square seal has been stamped through the glaze, bearing the characters *t'ien* (heaven) *hsin* (heart).
Probably northern Chinese: Sung dynasty.
H. 2 in.   D. 5⅝ in.

LUNG-CH'ÜAN WARE OR CELADON

253 Vase of rectangular form with pear-shaped outline and wide mouth: two square tubular handles. The body is a dark reddish brown ware of close, hard texture; and the glaze is thick, sparsely crackled, and of misty gray color warmed by the red tinge, which is partly due to the underlying clay appearing through it. The mouth is brown at the edge, where the glaze is thin. The base is hollow and pierced with two holes for a cord which would pass through the tubular handles above. There are large flaws on one side where the glaze has halted in its flow and congealed in large drops; and a few smaller flaws of the same kind occur elsewhere. This vase seems to correspond closely with the *fên ch'ing* colored type of Kuan ware, described in Chinese books as having a "brown mouth and iron foot," and a faint tinge of red in the glaze.
Kuan or Ko ware: Sung dynasty.
H. 16 in.   D. 11¼ in.

254 Vase, bottle-shaped, with pendulous body and wide, tapering neck: low foot with two openings at the sides. Dark red-brown stoneware with thick smooth glaze of *clair-de-lune* gray with wide-meshed irregular crackle of brown color. Under the base the glaze has run in thick, rounded folds like congealed fat.
Probably Ko ware: Sung dynasty.
H. 13⅜ in.   D. 8½ in.

255 Tall vase of oviform body with long, spreading neck. Grayish white porcelanous ware covered with olive-green celadon glaze, with metal bands where the three pieces of which the original consists join. The lowest division is regularly crackled; the two top ones are not. At the foot the earth has

slightly reddened and the base is covered with crackled celadon glaze.
Lung ch'üan ware: Sung dynasty.
H. 32½ in. D. 12½ in.

256 Vase with ovoid body, tall cylindrical neck with spreading mouth, and slightly spreading base. Gray-white porcelanous ware burnt rusty brown at the raw edge of the base and covered with a beautiful gray-green celadon glaze of faint bluish tone. On the body is a bold peony scroll in relief, and below it a belt of stiff plantain leaves carved in relief. On the neck are three peony sprays in relief between two bands of wheel-made ridges. The mouth has a metal band.
Lung-ch'üan ware: Sung dynasty.
H. 19½ in. D. 11 in.

257 Baluster-shaped vase of gray-white porcelanous ware reddened in the firing. Covered with fine grayish green celadon glaze. Decorated with a band of flowering branches; ribbed on the neck and fluted on the lower part. A waster found on the spot of the Lung-ch'üan kilns.
Lung-ch'üan ware: Sung dynasty.
H. 9⅝ in. D. 4⅛ in.

258 Fluted bowl of gray-white porcelanous ware, reddened in the fire. Covered with a fine blue-green celadon glaze. A waster found on the site of the Lung-ch'üan kilns.
Lung-ch'üan ware: Sung dynasty.
H. 3⅛ in. D. 5½ in.

259 Vase and cover of grayish white porcelanous ware reddened in the fire and covered with smooth gray-green glaze. Decorated with a dragon moulded in the round and encircling the neck; around the base is a band of formal leaves; on the cover is a squatting bird.
Lung-ch'üan ware: Sung dynasty.
H. 9¾ in. D. 5 in.

260 Pot; low, barrel-shaped. Grayish white porcelanous ware burnt red in the firing and covered with a blue-green transparent glaze accidentally crackled and decorated with a moulded pattern of a formal scroll of flowers and leaves

between two rows of knobs; simulated mask and ring handles.
Lung-ch'üan ware: Sung dynasty.
H. 6¼ in.   D. 9½ in.

261   Incense-burner of hard porcelanous ware burned red in the
firing.   Covered with a beautifully crackled blue-green glaze.
Lung-ch'üan ware: Sung dynasty.
H. 3¾ in.   D. 5½ in.

262   Shallow bowl with straight sides; of grayish white porcelanous
ware, covered with beautiful bluish green celadon glaze.   A
waster found on the site of the Lung-ch'üan kilns.
Lung-ch'üan ware: Sung dynasty.
H. 1⅞ in.   D. 5⅝ in.

263   Shallow bowl with gracefully fluted exterior.   Gray porcelanous ware burnt brown at the foot rim. The glaze is ice-
green celadon with complex crackle, and the surface has a dull
lustre and the texture of sugar icing.
Sung dynasty: perhaps Tung Ching ware made near K'ai-
fêng Fu.
D. 6⅜ in.

264   Bowl of conical shape, slightly rounded; light gray paste with
dull gray-green glaze over white slip.
Northern Chinese: Sung dynasty.
H. 2 in.   D. 5½ in.

265   Cup of conical shape with small foot.   Grayish white porcelanous ware, reddened in the firing and covered with a beautiful smooth gray-green glaze.
Lung-ch'üan ware: Sung dynasty.
H. 2 in.   D. 5 in.

266   Fluted bowl. Gray-buff ware covered with a thick green glaze,
regularly crackled; at the lip the clay has darkened in the
firing and shows through the glaze.
Celadon: Sung dynasty.
H. 4¾ in.   D. 9⅜ in.

267   Bowl of conical form with small foot. Gray porcelanous ware
with olive-green celadon glaze faintly clouded with gray.

Inside is a boldly carved scroll with a large peony flower and foliage. A wheel-made ring on the outside below the mouth. Probably northern Chinese: Sung dynasty.
H. 3½ in.   D. 8 in.

268   Bowl of globular form with spreading lip; the outside decorated with lotus leaves carved in the dark gray paste. A white slip was applied under the transparent olive-green glaze.
Corean or northern Chinese: Sung dynasty.
H. 2½ in.   D. 5⅜ in.

269   Fluted bowl of conical form, slightly curved sides, and small foot. Light gray porcelanous earth turned brown-red in the firing and covered with an olive-green celadon glaze.
Lung-ch'üan ware: Sung dynasty.
H. 3⅜ in.   D. 8 in.

270   Bowl of conical form with gently rounded sides and small foot. Gray porcelanous ware burnt red on the base rim. Beautiful ice-like glaze of deep celadon green with olive tone, sparsely crackled. The exterior is carved in shallow relief with petals suggesting a lotus flower. This bowl was excavated in Rhages, Persia.
Lung-ch'üan ware: Sung dynasty.
H. 4⅜ in.   D. 9⅜ in.

271   Fluted bowl of gray porcelanous earth covered with gray-green celadon. Found in Rhages, Persia, and dating in consequence from before the destruction of that town in 1256.
Lung-ch'üan ware: Sung dynasty.
H. 4 in.   D. 8 in.

272   Celadon shard of gray porcelanous earth covered with a gray-green celadon glaze; in design and texture almost exactly like 271.   Found on the site of the Lung-ch'üan kilns and brought over by Mrs. Rose Sickler Williams.
Lung-ch'üan ware: Sung dynasty.

273   Wine pot: globular, on three feet with erect handle in the form of a dragon ridden by a child (or demon). Grayish

white porcelanous ware carved with design of phoenixes and foliage and covered with a brown-green transparent glaze.
Lung-ch'üan ware: Sung dynasty.
H., with handle, 8¼ in.   D. 6¼ in.

274   Bowl of rounded shape with straight sides on a high foot. Hard gray ware covered with green glaze. Inside is a moulded design of figures in three panels; both inside and outside, a "cloud and thunder" border.
Lung-ch'üan ware: Yüan dynasty.
H. 4⅜ in.   D. 6⅜ in.

275   Bowl of conical form with wide mouth and small foot, the sides gently curving. Grayish porcelanous ware with ornament moulded in shallow relief under a transparent green celadon glaze of brownish tint which has run into a pool at the bottom inside. In the center is a geometrical quatrefoil design inclosing stiff foliage, surrounded by four formal flowers and leaves. Border of ovals inclosing lozenges. The outside is scored with radiating vertical lines.
Probably northern Chinese: Yüan dynasty.
H. 3 in.   D. 7⅛ in.

276-277   Pair of bowls of shallow conical form with small foot and wide mouth. Buff porcelanous ware with olive-green celadon glaze. The interiors are carved with a beautiful design of peony flowers and foliage shaded with combed lines. One has foliage on the exterior: sand-marks under the base.
This kind of ware is nearly related in style to the Corean.
Probably northern Chinese: Sung dynasty.
H. 2 in.   D. 6¼ in.

278   Wine jar with broad ovoid body, short neck, and wide mouth: the bottom is formed by a saucer which has been dropped into place, held in by the curve of the sides, and secured by the glaze. Gray porcelanous ware burnt rusty brown at the raw edges of the mouth and base. Celadon glaze with complex crackle: a wide straight mesh inclosing a small, irregular network of faint lines. The color inside is greenish gray with a tinge of blue; outside it is jade-green, and the surface is softened by decay.
Lung-ch'üan ware: Sung dynasty.
H. 10⅝ in.   D. 13½ in.

279 Shallow bowl. Gray porcelanous ware burnt red at the foot rim. The glaze is green celadon of bluish tinge. In the bottom of the bowl two unglazed fishes have been burnt a dark brown. Lung-ch'üan ware: Sung dynasty.
H. 2 in. D. 6¼ in.

280 Small, pear-shaped jar with wide mouth. Hard gray porcelanous ware burnt red and covered with crackled gray glaze. Celadon type: Sung dynasty.
H. 2⅜ in. D. 3¼ in.

COREAN WARE

281 Bottle with globular body and tall, slender neck of cylindrical form with a ring at the top. Gray porcelanous ware with inlaid ornament in white and black under a greenish gray celadon glaze faintly frosted with brown. On the sides are four sprays of alternating lotus and chrysanthemum; on the shoulder is a *ju-i* border; and there is a narrow band of key-fret at the mouth and an incised border of leaf and tongue pattern at the base.
Corean: Korai period.
H. 13 in.   D. 6½ in.

282 Ewer of double gourd form with long spout and twisted handle with knot-shaped ring. Gray porcelanous ware burnt red at the base: sparsely crackled celadon glaze covering lightly incised designs of lotus flowers on each side and cloud-scrolls on the neck.
Corean: Korai period.
H. 13 in.   D., with spout and handle, 9 in.

283 Ewer with pear-shaped body slightly flattened on the shoulders and moulded in shallow vertical lobes, plain spout, and grooved handle with ring to attach the cover. The latter is surmounted by a lotus flower, the petals modeled in full relief, in which a bird has settled. Gray porcelanous ware with crackled gray-green celadon glaze slightly frosted with brown. On the shoulders are lightly etched floral sprays. Spur-marks beneath.
Corean: Korai period.
H. 10½ in.   D., with spout and handle, 7 in.

284 Vase of oval form with small neck and low, cup-shaped mouth. Gray porcelanous ware of fine texture, burnt red at the base

and ornamented with a beautiful carved design under a soft greenish gray celadon glaze of bluish tone: two phoenixes (*fêng huang*) in a peony scroll with etched details covering the entire surface.
Corean: Korai period.
H. 11 in.   D. 7¼ in.

285   Baluster-shaped vase with small, short neck;   of gray porcelanous ware with inlaid decoration of flying herons and clouds, and covered with a green-gray celadon glaze.
Corean: Korai period.
H. 13¼ in.   D. 7½ in.

286   Vase and stand, the former of globular form with short, straight neck and narrow mouth.   Gray porcelanous ware with inlaid ornament in white and black under a partially crackled gray-green celadon glaze lightly frosted with brown.   On the sides are three large phoenixes (*fêng huang*) with scrolled tails and three peony sprays between.   Sand-marks underneath.   The stand is saucer-shaped, with a raised ring in which the vase fits, and four feet, each ornamented with a lion mask.
Corean: Korai period.
H. 8 in.   D. of vase, 8¼ in.   Total H. 11¼ in.

287   Wine pot with ovoid body, grooved handle with twig-shaped ring and Greek palmette attachment, spout with lotus-leaf moulding, and lotus-flower cover.   Gray porcelanous ware with soft greenish gray celadon glaze, lightly crackled.   On the body is a bold melon-vine scroll with large leaves, small blossoms, and tendrils reserved in a dark gray-green ground: the details throughout are finely etched in the paste.   The cover has radiating scrolls inlaid in white.   Spur-marks beneath.
Corean: Korai period.
H. 7 in.   D., with spout and handle, 8¾ in.

288   Wine pot with oval, melon-shaped body, plain spout, grooved handle with twig-shaped ring, and lotus-pattern cover.   Gray porcelanous ware with inlaid ornament in white and black under a smooth greenish gray glaze of bluish tone.   Lotus and chrysanthemum designs alternate on each lobe: below is a

border of carved leaf and tongue pattern, and on the shoulder is a band of petal ornament inlaid.
Corean: Korai period.
H. 8⅛ in.   D., with spout and handle, 8½ in.

289   Bottle with pear-shaped body, tall tapering neck, and spreading mouth.   Gray porcelanous ware with inlaid ornament in white and black under a smooth greenish gray celadon glaze of bluish tone, sparsely crackled and frosted in places by decay.   On the body are four medallions of lotus and chrysanthemum designs: between them are pendants of small circles hanging from a band of similar circles, the spaces filled with chrysanthemum sprays.   Below is a border of lotus petals, and above a band of chrysanthemum flowers.   On the neck are four tapering scrolls and a wave border.
Corean: Korai period.
H. 14 in.   D. 8 in.

290   Bulbous bottle with short neck and two small ring handles; of grayish porcelanous ware turned red in firing, with incised formal design and ribbed body covered with transparent celadon glaze.
Corean: Korai period.
H. 6 in.   D. 6¼ in.

291   Bottle in the form of a floating duck; dark gray paste reddened in the fire, covered with white slip in which the lines of the feathers and wings have been incised, the whole covered by a beautiful gray-green glaze, finely crackled.
Corean or northern Chinese.
L. 7½ in.

292   Bowl: flat, bulbous, with wide, flaring rim.   Gray porcelanous ware decorated inside with an engraved design of six flowers and a border of thunder pattern under a smooth gray-green celadon glaze of bluish tinge.   Six spur-marks under the covered base.
Corean: Korai period.
H. 3½ in.   D. 7⅛ in.

293   Bowl with small, flat foot and rounded sides.   Gray porcelanous ware covered with a gray-green celadon glaze of bluish

tinge. In parts covered with unintentional and large crackle. Three spur-marks under the covered base.
Corean: Korai period.
H. 3 in.   D. 8⅛ in.

294   Bowl of conical shape with rounded sides of hard buff ware covered with a bluish green transparent celadon glaze. Outside decorated with double rows of carved lotus leaves. The foot, covered with glaze, has three spur-marks.
Corean: Korai period.
H. 6¾ in.   D. 3¼ in.

295   White bowl of conical form with small foot. Thin porcelanous ware, burnt red at the unglazed base. Inside is engraved a design of boys and shell-like scrolls. Greenish transparent glaze, lightly crackled.
Corean: Korai period.
H. 2⅛ in.   D. 8 in.

296   Bowl with foot rim and slightly rounded sides. Gray porcelanous ware covered with a light brown celadon glaze evenly crackled. Decorated inside with a carved band of dragons and a lotus flower on the bottom. Three spur-marks on the covered base.
Corean: Korai period.
H. 3¼ in.   D. 6 in.

297   Saucer of white porous porcelanous ware with a thin greenish glaze, the broad rim unglazed. Decorated with slip design, ducks and fishes in a lotus pond. The thinly glazed base without spur-marks, fired right side up.
Corean: Korai period.
H. 1⅛ in.   D. 5⅜ in.

298   Saucer of white porcelanous earth with concave bottom and rim left unglazed. Covered with a white transparent glaze and decorated with a simple design of a dolphin. Found in Corea.
Pai Ting ware: Korai period.
H. 1 in.   D. 5⅜ in.

299   Ewer with melon-shaped body, high neck contracted in the middle, long spout, and flat handle with grooved edges and a

ring at the top. White porcelanous ware of porous-looking texture with thick cream-white glaze of Ting type, slightly crackled. A wheel-made ring on the neck below the lip. Sand-marks beneath.
This type belongs to the class of *haku-gorai*, or "white Corean."
Corean: Korai period.
H. 8⅝ in. D., with spout and handle, 5½ in.

300 Vase with oval, melon-shaped body, high neck with wide flaring mouth, and low foot moulded with leaf and tongue pattern. On the neck is a reeded band of slender leaf and tongue pattern. Translucent white porcelain with porous-looking body and pearly white glaze faintly browned by age. This rare and singularly beautiful vase recalls both Greek and Egyptian pottery in the details of its design.
Corean: Korai period.
H. 10¼ in. D. 6 in.

301 Dish in the shape of a six-petaled flower. Translucent white porcelanous ware entirely covered, except at parts of the rim, with a creamy white glaze showing the Ting tear drops. Fired right side up, but showing no sign of spur-marks though the base is entirely glazed.
Corean: Korai period.
H. 1¼ in. D. 6¾ in.

302 Small pot with cover of gray porcelanous ware with a smooth gray-green celadon glaze of bluish tinge. Three spur-marks under the partly covered base.
Corean: Korai period.
H. 1⅞ in. D. 3 in.

———

303 Bowl: conical with rounded sides; hard gray ware covered with a double slip, one rose-pink, the other white, and a greenish thin transparent glaze: inside, three spur-marks.
Tz'ŭ-chou type: Sung dynasty.
H. 3 in. D. 7⅛ in.

SCULPTURE AND BRONZES

304 Vase with two rows of figures in relief, representing mourners with a coffin, a table of offerings, and musicians. Hard grayish white stoneware fired dark reddish brown, with black glaze mottled and streaked witb brown.
Probably Wei dynasty.
H. 7⅛ in.   D. 6 in.

305 Pair of clasped hands, probably from an over-life-size Lohan. Hard, fine, yellowish white earth on a core of rough reddish clay.   Greenish white, thin, finely crackled glaze with brown weather stains.
Ascribed to the T'ang dynasty.
H. 7 in.   D. 4½ in.

306–307 Two figures of seated Lohans. Of reddish buff soft ware, covered with white slip and green and yellow glazes, the green finely crackled and in parts iridescent.
Attributed to the T'ang dynasty.
H. 9½ in.   W. 5½ in.

308 Horse's head: dark gray earth fired red and unglazed.
Han dynasty.
H. 8⅜ in.   D. 11 in.

309 Cock: reddish brown heavy clay, with no trace of glaze.
Early Han dynasty.
H. 6½ in.   D. 7 in.

310 Boar: gray clay without traces of glazing.
Early Han dynasty.
H. 5½ in.   D. 9½ in.

311 Prehistoric animal of soft reddish clay covered with white slip; the glaze has altogether disappeared.
Early Han dynasty.
H. 4½ in.   D. 7 in.

312 Rabbit of light buff clay, no slip, the glaze entirely disintegrated.
Early Han dynasty.
H. 4¾ in.   D. 7½ in.

313 Lion of buff clay covered with white slip, with traces of painting; the glaze has disappeared.
Han dynasty.
H. 2 in.   D. 4⅞ in.

314 Figure of a pawing horse, richly caparisoned, with saddle covered by a floating saddle-cloth. Traces of unfired coloring.
Han dynasty.
H. 15½ in.

315 Tomb figure: a tall lady with hands joined under a long scarf; of light buff soft ware slightly baked and decorated with unfired colors.
Han dynasty.
H. 12 in.   D. 3 in.

316 Tomb figure: a tall lady made of light soft ware slightly baked and decorated with unfired black lines.
Han dynasty.
H. 10 in.   D. 3 in.

317 Pair of tomb figures, each representing a tall lady with a green dress and orange scarf. Light buff clay slightly baked, the colors unfired.
Han dynasty.
Each: H. 10½ in.

318 Tomb figure: a lady sitting on the ground; of fine white clay covered with thin yellow glaze slightly fired and with a ribbon painted in brilliant red.
Han dynasty.
H. 5¼ in.

[67]

319 Tomb figure: a lady with long, flowing robes and curious horned head-dress, playing on a cymbal. Traces of unfired coloring.
Han dynasty.
H. 6¾ in. D. 3¾ in.

320 Running pig of white marble.
Han dynasty.
H. 1¼ in. D. 4½ in.

321 Figure of a seated kylin: stone of slate and yellow-brown color.
Han dynasty.
H. 11½ in. D. 7 in.

322 Figure of Kuan Yin, with richly ornamented halo and crown, seated on a throne beneath a conventionalized *bo* tree. Rectangular pedestal decorated in relief with adoring children on lotus flowers in a lotus pond. White marble with traces of polychromy.
Wei dynasty.
H. 13 in. D. 6½ in.

323 Stone sculpture in the form of a small stele. On the front is a seated Buddha with an ornamental halo incised with Buddha figures; beside him are two attendants on lotus buds. The back of the stele is decorated with incised designs in three rows, the upper one containing two figures making offerings to a central figure seated on a throne, the two lower ones, figures in arches. On the sides of the stele are dragons in low relief; the top has been broken off.
The inscription puts the date as 485 A. D.
Wei dynasty.
H. 12 in. W. 7 in.

324 Statue of Narayüen, protector of Buddha; white marble.
T'ang dynasty.
H. 26 in.

325 Standing figure of Buddha in white marble, the archaic folds of drapery showing strong Indian influence.
T'ang dynasty.
H. 41¼ in.

SCULPTURE AND BRONZES

326 White marble Buddha; standing figure in a simply draped robe; the hands are in the position of encouragement.
T'ang dynasty.
H. 38 in.

327 Black marble figure of Kuan Yin, richly dressed and jeweled. She holds in her left hand a lotus blossom, in her right a vase, and stands upon a double lotus throne.
Wei dynasty.
H. 44 in.

328 Stone figure of Kuan Yin, standing on a lotus throne holding in her hand a lotus flower; sculptured in full relief.
Wei dynasty.
H. 27 in.   W. 8⅝ in.

329 Stone figure of an adoring Bodhisattva kneeling with clasped hands on a double lotus throne.
T'ang dynasty.
H. 22½ in.

330 Stone slab, probably an altar frontal, carved in relief and pierced. In the center four Bodhisattvas standing on lotus flowers uphold and adore a lotus bud partly in the shape of an Indian stupa surmounted by a phoenix with halo and outspread wings. On the sides two haloed warriors are standing, one on two lions, the other on a tiger and a ram. Between these in each of two openwork panels two kneeling saints hold flaming jewels, while the space above these panels is filled in with rows of sitting figures in beaded circles and elaborate framework. The piece shows strong Indian and Persian influence.
T'ang dynasty.
H. 23½ in.   L. 7 ft. 7½ in.

331 Two stone slabs each elaborately carved with architectural border above a row of eight circles with beaded and carved frames, each circle containing a sitting figure. The figures show strong Persian influence and the style of both pieces is very like that of No. 330, although they do not fit the piece.
T'ang dynasty.
H. 7½ in.   L. 37½ in.

332   Semicircular stone slab on which is engraved a scene representing Buddha on a throne under a canopy preaching in a palm grove to a large gathering of Bodhisattvas, guardians of the lower world, angels, priests, and demons. The lower part is covered with a beautiful band of scrollwork.
T'ang dynasty.
H. 34 in. L. 4 ft. 6½ in.

333   Square stone slab carved with circular medallion containing a design, a seated Kuan Yin after Wu Tao Tzu, and three inscriptions translated as follows:
At the right: the picture of Buddha incised on stone was among the treasures of the Emperor Tai Tsung, of the T'ang dynasty. Together with the "Six Horses" and the "Chao Ling" picture, it was deposited in an old resting-place at Ku Kou. A farmer found it, and, thinking that it was only a square stone, took it home and gave it to his daughter as a stone on which she could wash clothes. She observed that the reflected light from the stone filled her whole room, and she continued to polish it until it was like gold. It became a family treasure, and she hid it away from those who came asking to see it. After I became Magistrate of this district, I found this stone in the village of Hsi Han. I presented it to the Pao Ning Temple on the fifteenth day of the ninth moon of the Kuei Mao year of K'ang Hsi (second year)— (A. D. 1663).
(Signed) Hsü K'ai-hsi, of Ho Hsui.
At the bottom:
Namah Kuan Shih Yin
In the beginning is Buddha
In the end is Buddha
Buddha and his Law have made me eternally happy in my serenity.
In the morning I think of Buddha
In the evening I think of Buddha
All my thoughts flow from my fortunate fate
In my rising thoughts Buddha is ever in my mind.
When I was wrapped in swaddling clothes and lost my beloved father I inquired in what way I could rescue him from purgatory and bring him to the heavenly heights. There was no other way than that of Buddha.
Recently I have acquired two pictures by Wu Tao Tsu of the T'ang dynasty. I gave instructions to have them copied on

stone by artisans, and have written a laud at the side of the pictures to perpetuate the record of them.

My desire is that all who see this picture and read my commendation of it should be spared the bitter experience of losing a father in youth.

Hsiao Sheng, 2nd year (A. D. 1095), Tsing Ming (Easter Day).

Written by Chao Hung, of Tien Hsui District.

Carved by Wei Ming, of Ch'i Yang.

At the left: a holy laud in praise of Kuan Shih Yin.

Sung dynasty. 1095 A. D.

Square, 20½ in.

334 Large fish bowl: semi-globular with flat lip and four mask and ring handles. Decorated inside with swimming ducks, fishes, and tortoises in relief; outside with three horizontal bands of ornament showing archaic hunting scenes separated by narrow bands of formal ornament. The decoration is incised and the incisions filled with a whitish paste. The handles are in the form of monster heads and the rings have incised ornament; around the foot rim is a plaited cord in relief.
Tsin dynasty, found in Si-An-Fu.
H. 11 in.   D. 20 in.

335 Bronze sacrificial vessel called "Yi." Deep body, wide mouth, four hollow cast handles surmounted by horned heads and with square drops. Body boldly decorated with Chou ornaments representing a head. Around the base an ornament of dragons in pairs repeated four times. Inscription incised in the bottom. Areas within and without of mirror-like surface.
Chou dynasty.
H. 8¼ in.   D. 9½ in.

336 Bronze sacrificial vessel called "Yi." Deep body, wide mouth, two loop handles with drops surmounted by rams' heads. Ram's head mask on each side amidst Chou ornament in shape of a dragon. Inscription on the bottom.
Chou dynasty.
H. 6¾ in.   D. 9 in.

337 Bronze sacrificial vessel, called "Yi," with two handles in the shape of peacocks. The body is decorated with Chou orna-

ment suggesting a face; the upper band, with archaic dragons. The bottom is curiously decorated with an animalistic design. The patina is bronze gilt with dark green and crimson corrosion. Inscription of eight letters on the bottom.
Chou dynasty.
H. 5¼ in. D. 7 in.

338 Bronze vase in the shape of a bottle of flat, circular form with short, round neck and square base. On the neck are loop handles and silver inlaid rings. Covered all over with a symmetrical pattern of silver inlay.
Han dynasty.
H. 12¼ in. D. 11 in.

339 Bronze sacrificial vessel called "Lai," of quadrilateral bulbous shape, square base and neck, with two ring and mask handles. The flat cover, with chamfered edges and surmounted by four erect rings, serves as a saucer. The ornament which covers the whole surface in geometrical design is inlaid with pieces of malachite stuck in a kind of composition; other parts are filled with bent and hammered metallic wire. The handles in the shape of dragons' heads are beautifully cast.
Han dynasty: found in 1913 in a ruined tomb near Yu-Ling-Fu, Shensi.
H. 20¼ in. D. 10⅛ in.

340 Bronze sacrificial vessel "Lai," in the shape of an eagle. The surface is covered with a beautiful incised ornament, the eyes inlaid with gold, as are four letters of early form on the comb. The beak is hinged so as to serve as a spout. From Tai-Yuan-Fu.
Late Chou dynasty.
H. 10½ in. D. 9 in.

341 Libation vessel in the form of a low, broad ewer, having at one end a handle in the shape of a horned monster and at the other a short spout. The vessel stands on three feet and has a flat, detached cover with a circular band of incised scrollwork; similar bands of ornament with a pointed edge border the lip and spout. The handle is moulded in relief and set with small turquoises. On the upper surface of the spout is a monster's head in low relief. The surface is covered with a

beautiful green patina of lacquer-like smoothness with a slight incrustation.
Chou dynasty.
H. 8½ in.   D. 12½ in.

342   Sarcophagus in reduced size, of gilt bronze: on a terrace with an openwork fence stands an altar supported by four guardians.   Upon this is a coffin with overhanging lid, decorated on the sides with dragons on clouds and a tiger; at the head is the red bird (of the morning), at the foot coiled serpents. Inside is a smaller coffin, also gilt, undecorated.
T'ang dynasty.
H. 14 in.   L. 13 in.

343   Masque of bronze gilt in the shape of a door knocker; supposed to be a coffin ornament.   Horned dragon head holding in its mouth a ring formed by two dragons holding the sacred jewel.
T'ang dynasty.
L. 13½ in.   D. 8 in.

APPENDIX

KERAMIC WARES OF THE SUNG DYNASTY

BY

ROSE SICKLER WILLIAMS

INTRODUCTION

IN presenting the following work to the public, the author desires to state that the period assigned for research, on a subject of such magnitude, was brief. It also was coincidental with the "Second Revolution" in China, and conditions have been somewhat unfavourable to scientific research. Nevertheless, it is believed that valuable sources of information have been unearthed, from which yet greater knowledge may be expected in the future.

The sincerest thanks of the author are due to the many friends who have aided in her investigations, both by submitting their collections for examination and by contributing information. The list is too long to be published; but special mention should be made of H. I. H. Prince P'u-lun, H. E. T'ang Shao-yi, H. E. Sheng Hsüan-huai, (Chao) Ch'ing K'uan, Hon. King Kung-pah of Peking, Dr. Chao S. Bok of Tangshan Engineering College, Mr. Chun Chik-yu of Hongkong, and Mr. Kuan Mien-chün of Peking. The unfailing and painstaking courtesy and kindness of these men, and their deep interest in the ancient arts of their country, promise much for the future of antiquarian research in China.

Hearty thanks are also due to Dr. Morrison for the free use of his unique library, which, we believe, contains practically all the books and pamphlets that have been published in English and French on the subject of Chinese pottery.

The native works consulted are the Hsiang Yüan-p'ien

Catalogue (in the original and in Dr. Bushell's translation), the T'ao Lu (in the original and in the French of Julien), the T'ao Shuo, and the Ko Ku Yao Lun. Citations from other Chinese works, which will be found in the text, are quoted in those above mentioned.

Among English writers consulted are Hirth, Bushell, Brinkley, Hippisley, and Hobson.

KERAMIC WARES OF THE SUNG DYNASTY

THE SUNG PERIOD

THE Sung dynasty was established in 960 A.D. by Chao K'uang-yin, who adopted the dynastic title of T'ai Tsu. His great task was to consolidate the empire after the confusion and military despotism of the Wu Tai, or Five Dynasties. During his reign, and that of his brother and successor Tai Tsung, this was fairly well accomplished, but the Empire of the Sungs was never at peace. The Kitan Tartars encroached upon it from the northeast, and the Kingdom of Hsia, led by a pretender of the imperial family, from the northwest. The Sungs were not successful warriors. They pursued a policy of compromise and retreat, sometimes making ignominious terms with their enemies, and finally, in 1126–27, falling back to the south of the Yangtse River and leaving the north in the possession of the Kin Tartars. Here, with the great river as a barrier, though still continually harassed by their enemies, they managed to maintain themselves on the throne until 1278.

But it is not with their military vicissitudes that we have to do. What interests us is that, in spite of these, they succeeded in making their period a golden age in China in philosophy, art, and literature. They produced the great historian Ssu-ma Kuang; the socialist reformer Wang An-shih, who lived to see his system cast down and discredited, but whose spirit still goes marching on; Chu Hsi, whose commentaries on the classical writings have been the standard of orthodoxy ever since his time; the inspired poet, statesman, and philosopher Su Tung-p'ei; the prince of painters Li Lung-mien; and a whole galaxy of immortals who may not be mentioned here. To the honour of the Sung rulers let it be said that, during their entire period, every phase of culture blossomed and bore fruit under the sunshine of imperial patronage. It was during their time that the Chinese potter rose from the rank of artisan to that of artist, and it is with this achievement that we have chiefly to deal.

CHINESE POTTERY BEFORE THE SUNG PERIOD

FOR the keramic products of the Chou and Han, see "Chinese Pottery of the Han Dynasty," by Berthold Laufer. This work is based on personal investigations made by the author from 1901 to 1904. The pieces described were mainly collected in Hsi-an Fu, province of Shensi, where they had been dug from graves of the Han period. They are all of the earthenware class, and the prevailing glaze is green.

Since Laufer's work was published, very extensive and important finds have been made, chiefly along the line of the Pien-Loh Railway in Honan. Peking is flooded with these specimens, as well as with clever imitations encouraged by the demand for the originals. The collection of these articles has become quite a vogue, both with Chinese and foreigners. They are well worthy the careful consideration of an expert, and demand a volume to themselves. Native connoisseurs believe that the Honan finds date from the Han downward through the Sung and Yüan, and hold that, in a general way, it is possible to approximate the date by the costuming of human figures, the character of the glazes, etc. Laufer's work does not give any human figures, and gives but a subordinate place to animals, though these form a very important part of the more recent discoveries. The various vessels, granary urns, stoves, etc., described by Laufer are now easy to procure in the Peking shops. It should not be very difficult to detect the imitations. Many of the mortuary pieces of a later date than the Han rise above the rank of earthenware.

Under the Wei dynasty (220–265) two old potteries are mentioned as having prepared ware for the service of the court. But probably the earliest kiln whose work rose above the quality of *wa*, or earthenware, was the Tung-ou, in what is now the province of Chehkiang. This work dates from the Tsin (265–419), and it is mentioned in the Ch'a Ching, or Tea Classic. The glaze was green.

Ching-tê-chên as a keramic centre began to attract attention as early as the beginning of the seventh century. The place was then known as Ch'ang-nan. A potter who worked there under the Sui (589–618) produced a green ware which obtained for its fabricator the sobriquet of *T'ao Yü*, or "Keramic Jade." It is said that the celadons had their origin in the attempts to imitate jade, and that white jade was the early ideal striven after in the white wares. At this early date the Ching-tê-chên (or rather the Ch'ang-nan) kilns were already distinguished by imperial patronage.

Under the T'ang dynasty we should mention the *Shou yao*, a yellowish ware made in the province of Anhui; the *Yüeh yao*, a greenish ware compared to ice and jade—a decided improvement on its predecessors, if we may judge by the enthusiastic comments of the Ch'a Ching and other old books; the *Shu yao*, a white ware made in Ssu-chuan and praised for its timbre; and lastly the *Pi-se yao*, or "secret colour ware," so called because it was reserved for imperial use. It resembled the Yüeh but was clearer and brighter. This ware was made under the patronage of the Ch'ien, a family that rose to power at the time of the decline of the T'ang, and having been assigned the principalities of Wu and Yüeh, ruled with their capital at Hang-chou for three generations, from 851 to 976, when they resigned their dominion to the Sungs.

But the greatest triumph of keramic skill previous to the Sung was the famous *Ch'ai yao*,[1] which supplied the model

---

[1] Since writing the above, H. E. T'ang Shao-yi has told me of a man in Foochow who claims to have a vase of Ch'ai in good condition. As there is no means of substantiating this statement, its chief interest lies in the extravagance of the claim, Chinese connoisseurs having long considered it difficult, if not impossible,

for many of the Sung productions. It was first made during the reign of Shih Tsung, of the later Chou (954–960), at Cheng-chou in Honan. At first it was called the "imperial ware," but afterward came to be known as *Ch'ai*, from the family name of the Emperor who ordered its manufacture. It is praised in the most extravagant terms by the old writers, and is said to have been *ch'ing* like the sky, clear as a mirror, thin as paper, and resonant as the musical stone, glossy, fine, and beautiful, with delicate markings and colouring, far surpassing in excellence everything that had preceded it. In this description we must, of course, make due allowance for the standard of comparison of the ancient writers. If it were possible now to discover and identify a surviving specimen, we should doubtless find it disappointing. But at the same time we are safe in assuming that, compared with its contemporaries and with all that had gone before, it was an easy leader. The praise lavished upon it spurred the potters of the Sung to their supreme efforts, and the colour designated for it by Shih Tsung, "the blue of the sky after rain," became the chief aim of all the Honan keramists.

FAMOUS KILNS OF THE SUNG DYNASTY

THE TING.

At Ting-chou, in the southern part of Chihli. In operation under the Northern Sung, probably from the beginning of the dynasty. Industry transferred to Ch'ang-nan when the capital was moved to the south, A.D. 1126–27.

THE JU.

At Ju-chou, in K'ai-fêng Fu. Established as supplementary to the Ting.

to find a piece of Ch'ai large enough to form a watch fob or a belt buckle. Mr. T'ang describes the piece as a melon-shaped vase about ten inches high, of a dark green colour like the shell of a crab, with small, regular, even crackle and a very thick glaze. This does not tally at all with our ideas of the Ch'ai as derived from literature and Mr. T'ang does not credit the assertion, though he considers the piece of great interest.

THE KUAN.

In the capital city of K'ai-fêng Fu. Established during the Ta Kuan period (1107). Transferred to Hang-chou when the court moved to the south.

THE LUNG-CH'ÜAN.

The Old Lung-ch'üan.

The Ko.

The Chang Lung-ch'üan.

At the village of Liu-t'ien, Lung-ch'üan district, Ch'u-chou prefecture, province of Chehkiang. The Liu-t'ien kilns were active from the beginning of the Sung, the "Old Lung-ch'üan" being their oldest wares, the "Ko" the most famous.

THE CHÜN.

At Chün-t'ai, also called Chün-chou, now Yü-chou, province of Honan. In operation from the beginning of the Sung.

THE CHIEN.

At Chien-chou, now Chien-yang district, Chien-ning prefecture, province of Fukien.

THE TING

I HAVE found no native work which fixes the date of the opening of the Ting kilns. The T'ao Lu tells us merely that they were in operation "during the Sung dynasty." We know, however, that even as far back as the T'ang (618–905) south Chihli was a keramic centre, and that the ware there produced was white, or of a yellowish tint which was then the nearest approach to it. It is said of the Hsing T'ai ware that it was of fine and glossy pâte, and the Ch'a Ching compares the tea bowls to silver or to snow, holding them inferior, however, to those of Yüeh (in Chehkiang), the latter being green and compared to ice and jade. Now Hsing T'ai is the head district of Shun-te Fu, midway between Ting-chou and Tz'u-chou.

We may well believe that its kilns supplied the type, and that it was their development which later produced the incomparable Ting and the fine white ware of Tz'u-chou.

According to the T'ang Shih Ssu K'ao, the Ting kilns turned out their best pieces during the Cheng Ho-Hsüan Ho period (1111–26). We are told that the production of the Ting type of ware was carried on at Ch'ang-nan after the transfer of the Sung capital to the south. Through the kindness of Mr. D. Lattimore, of Pao-ting Fu Provincial College, I obtained a copy of the Ting-chou Annals, expecting them to be a mine of information on the subject, particularly as the old kilns constitute the city's only claim to fame; but the only thing that rewarded my search was the bald statement that "once the kilns of Ting-chou were very famous and their products eagerly sought after by connoisseurs." Several Ting-chou students at the college were questioned on the subject. They had all heard of the kilns, but did not know just where they are supposed to have been located. One of the teachers, however, stated that the Ting pottery was very famous under the Sung and *before*, and that tradition has it that this pottery was made at a place called *Pai-t'u Ts'un*, or "Village of White Clay," somewhere to the west of the city. He added that no pottery is made there now. It ought not to be difficult to locate this place definitely; and as it appears never to have been exploited, it is possible that excavations there might be richly rewarded. Even broken pieces of genuine northern Ting are now of great interest and value.

The pâte of the best Ting ware was very fine and tender. It was of light grey colour, showing none of the purple-brown or iron tints of the other notable Sung wares, either before or after firing. It was manipulated with great delicacy, and some of the pieces were almost as thin as modern egg-shell. It was resonant, and while usually opaque was in certain instances slightly translucent. Brinkley calls it "a fine stoneware or semi-porcelain"; Dillon, "proto-porcelain or kaolinic stoneware." Native authorities do not raise the question. They call it *tz'u*, but, as I shall point out elsewhere, this term is not necessarily synonymous with our word "porcelain," no matter how the ideograph may be written. The exact composition of the Ting pâte can be determined only by analysis of existing specimens, and authenticated specimens of northern Ting are far too rare and valuable to be subjected to such a process. Our best hope of accurate knowledge on this subject lies in the excavations which may be made in the future at the "Village of White Clay."

The Ting glazes were white, purple, and black, the white being the type and by far the most important. An extract from the poem of Su Tung-p'e, to the effect that "the flower vases of Ting-chou were like carved red jade," is made authority for the statement that the Ting kilns produced a red ware also. But if such a ware ever existed, it is negligible for our purpose, as the collector will never meet with it. The Hsiang Catalogue (Illustrated Description of the Celebrated Porcelain of Different Dynasties), translated by Dr. Bushell, gives twelve Ting pieces, of which five are purple. From this it would appear that in Hsiang's day (sixteenth century) purple pieces were comparatively numerous. They do not seem to have been imitated, however. I have met with no purple specimens of the Ting type, and the term *Ting yao* nowadays always implies a white ware. As for the black, Hsiang says it was very rare, and this was undoubtedly true as applied to the finer work. I am inclined to think, however, that some recently discovered specimens of black ware may be classed as *t'u Ting* and referred to the south Chihli kilns.

As compared with other notable Sung wares, the glaze of the white Ting was thin, "like a thin coat of cream," some one has said, and this comparison gives a very good idea of its appearance. In old Chüns and celadons the glaze has much body and is frequently found collected in masses near the bottom of the piece. While the glaze of the white wares is like cream, that of the coloured monochromes is like paste.

[87]

This contrast may be easily seen by comparing the piece of white Sung shown in the exhibit with the pieces of Yüan tz'u and Lung-ch'üan. In these latter the glazes form an appreciable part of the thickness of the piece.

The T'ao Lu, in speaking of Ting wares of the finest quality, says: "This ware was commonly called *fen Ting* (rice-flour Ting) and also *pai Ting* (white Ting)." It appears, however, that it is only the latter term which should be applied to the fine product of the northern kilns. The term *fen Ting* implies a tinge of buff in the glaze, and this was a characteristic of the later Kiangsi product. The *pai Ting*, however, was not a pure white like the *t'o t'ai* wares of the Yung-lo period. It was of a mellow, creamy tone, wonderfully soft and of great beauty.

Decoration was of various sorts. It was sometimes lightly incised under the glaze, sometimes printed or pressed on with a mould, and sometimes in pronounced relief. Another style of decoration called *hsiu* is not well understood. (See note to translation.) There were also perfectly plain pieces. The Ko Ku Yao Lun and the T'ang Shih Ssu K'ao unite in pronouncing the pieces having incised decoration the finest, and in giving second rank to the plain ones. It will be easily understood that those having sufficient body to carry decoration in pronounced relief could not compare with the others in delicacy, though the decoration itself was very often intricate and effective and the technique excellent. In the Catalogue of the Major Collection is found the statement that the Ting wares sometimes carried decoration in brown, as did the products of the kilns of Tz'u-chou. This does not seem at all unlikely, as the kilns of the two districts operated at the same time and turned out products similar in many respects, but I have not been able to confirm the statement by any native authority. If convinced that decoration in colour was ever employed, I should be inclined to apply to it the word *hsiu* above mentioned. Chinese scholars whom I have consulted are of the opinion that it means "painted."

The books tell us that the patterns most commonly used in decorating the Ting were peonies, day lilies, and flying phœnixes. (For the symbolism of these, see note to the translation of the T'ao Lu.) But these by no means monopolise the field. Like most of the famous Sung wares, the early Ting was modelled on old bronzes, and all the archaic designs found on such bronzes were faithfully reproduced. (For an example of this, see the magnificent purple censer shown in the Hsiang Catalogue.) The key-pattern and scroll-work of various sorts were widely used, particularly in incised decoration. I have seen two pieces showing a pair of fishes in the bottom, a style mentioned in literature as characteristic of the Old Lung-ch'üan wares. One of these pieces was held by the dealer to be a *t'u Ting*, possibly dating from the Sung, while the other was admittedly a Tao Kuang imitation made at the Kiangsi kilns. This is a very old pattern, and was undoubtedly much used on the Ting wares as well as on the Lung-ch'üan.

Several native works, in discussing the *pai Ting*, mention the occurrence of globules in the glaze, which they compare to tear-marks and which are spoken of as increasing the value of the piece in the eyes of connoisseurs. We can hardly believe that they were real embellishments or that they were intentional on the part of the potter. But, being a defect characteristic of early wares, they have come to be prized as an evidence of age. Brinkley believes, too, that they would be most likely to occur on pieces of greatest delicacy.

Bowls and plates of Ting were stoved in an inverted position, so that, unlike most Sung wares, the bottoms were perfectly glazed, while the rims were left exposed and afterward finished with bands of copper or silver. This is believed to constitute an important mark of authenticity, as it is held that the Ching-tê-chên kilns did not imitate it. It should be borne in mind, however, that there was no impossibility in their doing so, had they really wished to deceive, and for this reason the glazed bottom and copper rim must not be

[89]

considered absolute proof of the Sung origin of a piece. Let it be said, however, in justice to the Ching-tê-chên potters of the Ming, that for the most part their aim was not deception or slavish imitation, but the development and improvement of the type set for them by the northern kilns. Their work was of a quality which had no reason to fear comparison, and perhaps they did not use the copper rims simply because they had learned to finish the piece properly without them.[1]

The Ting kilns put forth a great variety of articles. Plates and saucers of various sizes and wide-mouthed bowls were common. There were many censers, tripods, and vases, closely imitating the old bronzes. In addition the T'ao Shuo gives us a list of flower vases and small objects for use in the library of the scholar, such as pencil rests, water basins for washing brushes, and small pots to contain water for the ink slab, designed in imitation of various natural objects, such as melons, egg-plant, camels, and even toads. These all occurred in the Ting wares, though they seem to have been more common in the heavier *Kuan* and *Ko*.

VARIETIES AND IMITATIONS OF THE TYPE

THE *t'u Ting* is a variety of the ware heavier, coarser, and more yellowish in colour than the *pai Ting* or *fen Ting*. From the text of the T'ao Lu one gathers that it was simply an inferior output made at the same kilns and at the same time as the other. And it seems but natural that from the very first pieces of varying degrees of fineness and excellence should have been produced, adapted to various uses and put upon the market at different prices. Or perhaps, while the finer wares were reserved for imperial use, the heavier work alone was put upon the market. The T'ao Shuo and the older works from which it quotes do not mention the *t'u Ting*. Brinkley, in Chapter III, "Wares of the Sung Dynasty," says: "There

---

[1] Mr. T'ang Shao-yi has since told me that under the Ming and later the copper rims were considered in bad taste.

was also produced at the same factory, during the Sung dynasty, a coarser species called the *t'u Ting yao.*" But in Chapter XII, "Chinese Pottery," he says that the *t'u Ting* was "an imitation of the celebrated Ting ware of the Sung," and he adds that the heavier examples came from the Kuang-tung factories. In describing these he says that they have "a paint-like, creamy glaze of varying thickness and lustre, its buff colour often showing tinges of blue." I have seen numerous specimens in shops and private collections, some of them quite creamy enough to have issued from the northern kilns, and others somewhat buff but showing no special tinge of blue. Moreover, they are sufficiently heavy and durable to have survived usage and transfer and to have undergone processes of burial and resurrection. One would like to believe that some of them, at least, are what they seem. It is an interesting point, for if they are genuine relics of the Sung kilns their analysis would teach much concerning the nature of the Ting pâte and glazes, for these heavy wares probably differed from the others more in technique and manipulation than in the nature of the materials used.

We have seen that with the transfer of the Sung capital to the south (1126–27) the manufacture of the Ting type of ware became centred at Ch'ang-nan, the world-famed Ching-tê-chên, where kilns had already been in operation from the seventh century. Doubtless the more skilled of the operators of the northern kilns went to Ching-tê-chên at this time, taking their skill and their traditions with them. We need look for no falling off in technique, but naturally different materials came into use. If, however, the peculiar keramic properties of the Ching-tê-chên *kao-lin* had then been discovered, the discovery was not applied to this species of manufacture. The T'ao Lu tells us that the Ch'ang-nan potters used powdered *ch'ing-t'ien* stone in making their biscuit. Whatever this may have been, it did not produce so fine, close-grained a pâte as the material procured from the "Village of White Clay." Just what occurred to produce the change in the colour of the glaze from a creamy white to a buff tinge is another point unelucidated, but from this time onward the manufacture of Ting wares went on at Ch'ang-nan without interruption.

Changes of dynasty did not put out the fires of the Ching-tê-chên kilns. Under the Mongol masters of the Yüan (1206–1341) they went on producing pieces which old-time native connoisseurs admit to be undistinguishable from the southern ware of the Sung. The Ko Ku Yao Lun tells us, however, that under the Yüan the best pieces were marked with the characters "Shu Fu," indicating their imperial destination. Under the Ming white wares of hard paste porcelain were made, but the manufacture of the soft paste Ting type was also kept up. Under Wan Li (1573–1620) the expert Hao Shih-chiu is said to have copied a Sung Ting tripod so successfully that the owner of the original could not tell which was his. As already mentioned, we have seen a handsome piece of the Ting type which was admitted by the dealer to be as late as Tao Kuang.

So much for the Ching-tê-chên kilns. And, as will be seen in the section devoted to supplementary kilns, the Ting wares were imitated with more or less success by the potter Shu of Chi-chou and his daughter Shu Chiao, by the potter P'eng Chün-pao of Ho-cho-chou, and by many others. All these varieties add to the confusion of the collector. True, the genuine northern Ting had characteristics which set it apart from all the others, but it is hardly an exaggeration to say that its safest distinguishing feature is the fact that it is no longer to be found.

EXAMPLES OF THE TING WARES

BUSHELL's "Chinese Art," Fig. 8, shows two Ting vases classed as Sung. These are in the Bushell collection.

At the Shanghai Exhibition, 1908, was shown a piece in the form of a boat with a child in it. It has an incised key-pattern border. Length, 7 inches; height, 2 inches. It was from the collection of Wang K'ai-zur and was classed as Sung *fen Ting*.

At the same exhibition were shown a pair of vases classed as *fen Ting*. These have a creamy, crackled glaze, with dragon and flying phœnix decoration. From the collection of A. W. Bahr. Probably early Ming.

At the Burlington Fine Arts Exhibition was shown a saucer-shaped dish with six-foil rim finished with a band. The ornaments are in low relief. There is a vine in the centre, and the six radiating compartments of the sides are decorated with peonies and other flowers. The border is of the design known as the silk-worm scroll. This piece was loaned by Mrs. Bushell.

The same exhibition showed a bottle of *t'u Ting* with creamy-white crackled glaze, "garlic-shaped" mouth, and archaic dragon and pearl in relief around the lower part of the neck. Decoration of scroll-work on the body.

Three vases of the *t'u Ting* type recently left Peking. The purchaser classed them as Sung. Their solidity and crackled glaze place them in the *t'u Ting* class, but they are finely finished and of excellent technique. The best of the three has a creamy glaze with only a slight tinge of buff, and decoration in low relief, evidently copied from an old bronze. A key-pattern scroll extends twice round the neck and down the sides. The crackle is of the fine fish-roe type. It may be a Ming product of the Ching-tê-chên kilns, but on this point it is impossible to speak with certainty. Analysis of the glaze would probably show lead. The very excellence of such a specimen leads one to doubt its age.

In the collection of General Munthe are three vases of the *t'u Ting* type. Two of these have the "garlic-shaped" mouth and dragons coiled about the neck. A third has a deeper tinge of buff than the others, with decoration of peonies incised under the glaze. This latter has a completely glazed bottom. These are all of heavier material and coarser workmanship than the three mentioned above.

[93]

At the Ta Chi Chang curio shop on the Ha-ta-men Street I saw a specimen of the finer Ting. It is a wide-mouthed bowl, very light and delicate but quite opaque. It has the hexagonal division of the sides, like the bowl mentioned above from the collection of Mrs. Bushell. The only decoration is an incised lotus at the bottom. The rim is unglazed and finished with a copper band. The dealer seemed ignorant of the origin and character of this piece.

The same dealer showed me a large plate of the *t'u Ting* type. It has a deeper tinge of yellow and is heavier than the bowl, but is still quite delicate. It also is finished with the copper rim. There are two fishes in the bottom and elaborate decoration in relief round the sides. Like the bowl just described, it has all the characteristics of genuine Sung ware, unless it lacks such as must be determined by analysis. But it requires great optimism to believe that pieces so fragile and of a shape so easily destroyed have survived from so remote a period.

Heavy pieces of the *t'u Ting* type, mostly vases, may be found in various shops on the Liu-li-ch'ang. If asked their origin, the dealer will usually say "Honan" and add that they are "out of the earth." It is quite true that recent railway construction has led to numerous finds of ancient pottery; and as these pieces are very solid, it is not unreasonable to suppose that some of them, at least, actually date from the Sung dynasty.

HINTS TO THE COLLECTOR

"THE best Ting was of the Cheng Ho–Hsüan Ho periods, but it is no longer found in *heaps*." (Ko Ku Yao Lun, 1387.)

"One does not see many Sung wares nowadays. The broken shards that remain are worth their weight in gold and jade." (Foreword of the T'ao Shuo, Ch'ien Lung period.)

The above two quotations, one written about one hundred and fifty and the other more than five hundred years ago, might seem to close the question to all but purely academic interest. Nevertheless, there are certain recent developments which may serve to justify the collector of Sung wares in his enthusiasm, particularly with regard to the heavier varieties. These are the excavations which have accompanied modern mine-opening and railway-building in China, and the wars and political upheavals which have caused princely and other wealthy families to put their hitherto jealously guarded heirlooms upon the market. It is asserted, too, that during and since Boxer times some of the imperial hoards have been rifled by their guardians and put into circulation.

THE JU

JU-CHOU is in the province of Honan, in the valley of the Ju River, some fifty miles west of the Ching-Han Railway line and to the southeast of Honan Fu. It is in the same general keramic district as Yü-chou, where the famous Sung Chün wares were made. The T'ao Lu tells us that it was under the direct jurisdiction of the capital, Pien-liang. (Bushell errs in saying that it is now Ju-chou Fu. It is not a prefectural city.)

Brinkley makes the statement that the Ju kilns were opened in 1130, which was three years after the transfer of the Sung capital to the south, but they are actually mentioned in a work written some years before. He appears to be quoting the T'ao Lu, though not literally, as follows: "The T'ao Lu says that the glaze of the *Ting yao* was often disfigured by fissures and other faults due to imperfectly prepared materials or unskilled stoving. These blemishes proved so embarrassing and unavoidable that in 1130 A.D. imperial orders were issued for the establishment of a special factory at Ju-chou, in the province of Kiangsu."

The only statement that I have been able to find in the T'ao Lu in any way resembling this is the following: "Ju was under the jurisdiction of Pien. The Sung (emperors), holding that the white Ting ware was in many ways unsuitable, ordered the opening of kilns at Ju for the manufacture of celadon (*ch'ing*)." This text does not mention the date, and unless there be direct literary evidence to the contrary, I should place the opening of the kilns at a date somewhat earlier than that assigned by Brinkley. The Sung emperors transferred their capital to the south in 1126–27, and we have already seen that at that time the manufacture of the Ting type of ware was removed to Ching-tê-chên. We shall also see that the *Kuan*, or imperial kilns, were then transferred from the old capital to the new. At a time when circumstances necessitated the closing of the other northern kilns it is not likely that new ones would have been opened in Honan, in close proximity to the Chin Tartars, before whom the Sung were receding; for, as we know, Ju-chou is in Honan, not, as Brinkley states, in Kiangsu.

The Ju-chou kilns are in operation to-day, and I find no evidence to show that they have ever been entirely closed. Richard's geography says: "The environs were formerly very industrial, but have lost their activity. The manufacture of common pottery is still carried on and gives the place some importance." Nevertheless, fine old Ju wares of the Sung are exceedingly rare. As they were not so fragile, the only explanation seems to be that the output, while under imperial patronage, was small. If such patronage were withdrawn with the transfer of the capital to the south, an immediate deterioration of the work would have resulted. In the absence of evidence I cannot contend that such was the history of the Ju-chou kilns, but offer it merely as a working hypothesis. There may be evidence in Chinese literature which has not come under my notice.[1]

[1] Dr. Chao S. Bok, himself a lineal descendant of the Sung imperial family and deeply interested in their history, informs me that the kilns at Ju-chou were not established by imperial order, but as the private enterprise of a prince of the ruling house. He has promised to secure for me the name of this prince and the exact date of the establishment of the kilns. He believes that they did not operate for a very long time, but that during their operation a very ardent competition existed between them and the Ting-chou factories, particularly with regard to the production of new colours in the glaze.

We are told that the pâte of the Ju was fine and glossy and shone like copper. This seems to indicate a reddish tinge in the clay even before firing. The wares varied in thickness. If any specimens ever equalled the Ting in delicacy, they have not survived.

The superiority of the Ju wares was entirely in the glaze, which was glossy and thick like congealed lard. To reproduce a colour like that of the famous old Ch'ai wares of the later Chou seems to have been the main object in the opening of the kilns. The T'ao Lu states that the colour was to be *ch'ing*, but it specifies "the *ch'ing* of the sky after rain." This expression naturally suggests blue, and observation bears out the rendering. I have heard it applied by dealers to pieces which, to my eyes at least, were frankly blue with no tinge of green. It is the colour of the modern Ju-chou ware to be found in abundance in Peking to-day. When a Chinese says of an object that it is "*ch'ing* like the sky," he does not mean the same thing as when he says "*ch'ing* like an onion." I asked a Chinese gentleman the colour of the pale blue silk gown that he wore, and he responded promptly "pale *ch'ing*."

So much for the term. But we must not be surprised when confronted by the fact that the colour of the Ju wares was not always the same. The skill of the old potters was purely empirical. They could rarely duplicate their wares. The colour of the sky after rain may have been always the colour aimed at, but many attempts produced a bluish green, or sometimes a green with no tinge of blue. Of the three Ju pieces which are figured in the Hsiang Catalogue (if the colours of the reproduction which I have seen are to be trusted), one is quite blue, one a celadon with a slight tinge of blue, and one with blue predominating but bearing a tinge of green. Before leaving this puzzling question of colour, we should mention that the T'ao Shuo quotes the Liu Ch'ing Jih Cha as saying that there was a yellowish tinge in the Ju glazes, and the Po Wu Yao Lan as comparing them in colour to egg-white. The author of the T'ao Shuo, commenting on this,

[97]

remarks that while the two statements seem to disagree, the general indication is that the colour was a pale *ch'ing*. Evidently this latter overworked word appeals to the Chinese mind as a safe resort in all disputes with regard to colour.

The T'ao Lu says that the Ju was sometimes uncrackled, sometimes with the fish-roe variety of crackle. The Ko Ku Yao Lun also refers to certain markings designated as "crab's claw" and "*Tsung yen*" or "coir-palm eyes." The first may refer to the larger variety of crackle, such as is shown by one of the Ju pieces in the Hsiang Catalogue. The latter term I have discussed in the note to the annexed translation. Native authorities do not agree as to its meaning. One man assured me that it is common colloquial usage, meaning "little holes." Another says that it is applied to certain markings on plants, not necessarily the palm. He pointed out such marks on a bamboo. They are not unlike eyes, and one can understand how such markings might accidentally occur on porcelain. I have seen no specimens, however, and have not heard the term used by dealers or connoisseurs. Whatever these markings were, it is obvious that they were not intentionally produced and were not originally regarded as embellishments.

A quotation from the Cho Keng Lu refers to sesame flowers on the bottom of Ju wares, which, if I understand the passage aright, appeared as though picked out with a small pointed instrument. No reference is made to this elsewhere.

Of the composition of the Ju glazes the books tell us only that powdered cornelian was added. I am not aware that this statement was made with reference to any other of the Sung wares.

The archaic decorations of the old bronzes were reproduced on the Ju wares. So far as I have been able to discover, the Ju is known only in vases. If bowls, plates, and the utensils of the library were made, as in the other Sung wares, they have not survived even in literature. The author of the T'ao Shuo speaks of "one small jar" which he was fortunate enough to see in the collection of a friend. It appears to have been the characteristic of cornelian in the glaze which most struck him, for he makes this the heading of his remarks. He says that such pieces were meant for imperial use and were "exceedingly hard to obtain."

IMITATIONS

THE Annals of Fu-liang tell us that the pâte and glaze of the Ju wares were imitated at Ching-tê-chên. These products probably excelled their originals in technique, but fell below them in depth and softness of glaze.

Modern wares from the Ju-chou kilns are for sale in Peking. At the Industrial Exposition Building I saw, among other articles, a large Ju censer. The colour is "the blue of the sky after rain." These pieces are not meant to deceive, and could not possibly do so. Still, they are not without decorative merit, and are of interest as marking the persistence of an old industry which may yet have a future.

EXAMPLES OF SUNG JU

SINCE the Hsiang Catalogue could figure only three pieces, and the author of the T'ao Shuo knew only one small jar, we must not expect much in the way of existing specimens.

HINTS TO THE COLLECTOR

FROM what has already been said it will be understood that the interest of the collector in this type of ware is largely theoretical. It is possible that a craze for Sung Ju may some day create a supply; but if so, no thinking person could take the matter seriously. A description of this ware has been necessary here, merely for the sake of symmetry and completeness in summarising the famous products of the dynasty.

Nevertheless, it is likely that a few specimens do exist in

private collections, and that they may yet fall under the eye of the collector. Such specimens may have found their way to America already, for undoubtedly the recent upheavals in China have caused the dispersal of collections of great merit.

Let the collector remember that, to be considered at all as a Sung Ju, the piece must be of fine, glossy, copper-coloured pâte, the glaze must be thick and unctuous, the colour blue, green, or a blending of the two with either predominating. It may be crackled or plain. The style should be archaic. The glaze is likely to terminate in a wavy line, and a portion of the lower part is very likely to be unglazed. Too great excellence of technique will indicate a Ching-tê-chên origin of later date than the Sung. But when all these characteristics are granted, I can find nothing which absolutely distinguishes it from other celadons, particularly the Kuan. If the presence of cornelian in the glaze could be proved, this would appear to clinch the argument. But probably the use of this material is only a tradition.[1]

THE KUAN

THE Kuan Yao were the Government kilns, properly speaking. They differed from the others in being set up at the capital and being more directly under the jurisdiction of the palace authorities. But we must not suppose that they were the only kilns which supplied ware for imperial use, or that their output was necessarily superior to that of other famous kilns, such as the Ting and Ju. In fact, the T'ao Lu tells us that such was not the case. I have noted in my researches that the term *Sung Kuan yao* as used to-day does not necessarily mean the product of these, strictly speaking, imperial kilns, but is used to indicate all Sung wares whose quality indicates that they were meant for palace use.

[1] Since writing the above I have been informed by H. E. T'ang Shao-yi that there is in his own collection a piece which he is strongly inclined to classify as Ju.
The collection of Mr. Ch'ing K'uan also contains a vase which he calls a Ju. It is beaker-shaped and of archaic appearance. The colour is a grey green and there is medium-sized crackle.

The books are quite definite as to the history of the Kuan kilns. They were opened during the Ta Kuan–Cheng Ho period. These are both designations of the reign of the Emperor Hui Tsung, and the time was 1107-18. During the latter year Hui Tsung, though still on the throne, again changed his *nien hao*. The kilns continued to operate at K'ai-fêng Fu until the transfer of the capital to the south, when they were closed and "interior kilns," or official kilns, were set up in the immediate precincts of the palace at Hang-chou. We have thus a period of only twenty years for the operation of the northern kilns.

As for the pâte of the Kuan, we are told that it was fine and glossy and that the wares showed the red mouth and iron foot, though whether this was before or after firing is not quite clear. There must have been considerable difference between the clays used in the north and in the south, and with regard to the latter the T'ao Shuo is more explicit. Quoting the Po Wu Yao Lan, it says: "The earth at the foot of Phœnix Hill, near Hang-chou, is reddish, so that the bottom of vessels made of it look like iron. This is commonly called 'the red mouth and iron foot.' For the glaze has a tendency to run down, away from the mouth of the vessel, leaving this or unglazed patches like the bottom in colour. But it is the iron foot which is most esteemed. There is no other clay which equals that of Phœnix Hill in this respect."

From this it would appear that in the southern wares the pâte was red before firing. I am inclined to think that the pâte of the northern Kuan, and of Honan wares generally, was dark, though not so markedly red as that of Hang-chou.

With regard to the thickness of the biscuit, there does not appear to have been much difference between the Ju and the Kuan. Of the former we are told that the wares were "of varying thickness"; of the latter, that "the body was thin." The Liu Ch'ing Jih Cha says of the Kuan that "those which were thin like paper were similar to the Ju and of equal value." In estimating remarks like this we must always bear in mind the standards of comparison of those early times, else we shall form a very exaggerated idea of the delicacy of the old wares.

The Ju appears to have excelled the Kuan in quality of glaze. We have seen the former characterised as very thick and unctuous and compared to lard. The latter is not described except as regards colour. This, the T'ao Lu says, was a *ch'ing* of varying depth. During the Ta Kuan period moon-white and bright green were also made. Generally speaking, this celadon appears to have shown less of the blue tinge than did the Ju. As to crackle, the T'ao Lu says that it showed the crab's-claw markings. The Po Wu Yao Lan adds to this that the starred-ice, eel's-blood crackle was the best, and the black plum-blossom crackle next in rank. This refers to the practice of rubbing red or black colouring matter into the crackle. This process is described in the section on Minor Kilns, under the heading "Sui Ch'i Yao."

Decoration appears to have been sparingly used on the Kuan wares, the pieces relying for their beauty on the quality of the glaze and the coloured crackle. The Hsiang Catalogue figures a tripod having the "t'ao-t'ieh," or ogre's head, in relief, and the "lei-wen," or thunder-scroll decoration. Other pieces are perfectly plain. We do not read or hear of plates or bowls with incised patterns of flowers, etc., as in the Lung-ch'üan celadons.

The Hsiang Catalogue shows us censers, tripods, libation cups, etc., in the Kuan wares. We also learn from the Catalogue, and from the list of articles given in the T'ao Shuo, that these kilns produced cups, watering pots, basins for washing brushes, ink palettes, brush rests, seals, and doubtless all the little articles so highly prized in the study of the Chinese scholar.

VARIETIES AND IMITATIONS

WE have seen that the transfer of the kilns from K'ai-fêng Fu to Hang-chou necessitates differentiation between the northern and the southern Kuan.

The T'ang Shih Ssu K'ao says that "a false Kuan was made at Lung-ch'üan." There seems, however, no good reason for assuming that the Lung-ch'üan celadons were at any time a conscious imitation of the Kuan, particularly with any attempt to deceive, though the similarity in the wares may have led to some confusion. The same authority says that the "secret colour" wares of Yü Yao, of the southern Sung, were often mistaken for the Kuan.

Some of the minor kilns turned out products similar to the Kuan, while the Ching-tê-chên factories have at various periods produced wares closely resembling them.

EXAMPLES OF SUNG KUAN

IT is only quite recently that native or foreign collectors have taken an interest in these products of the Sung imperial factories, or have differentiated them from other and similar celadons of corresponding date. Therefore, both in China and abroad there may be Kuan pieces which are not so classed. The term *Kuan yao*, as used in Peking, means the output of the imperial Ching-tê-chên factories, from the Ming downward, whereas *Sung Kuan yao* means any high-class Sung ware, presumably made for imperial use. Intelligent and enthusiastic native collectors are just awakening to the fact that an old celadon gains in interest and value if it possesses characteristics which refer it to the K'ai-fêng or Hang-chou imperial kilns.

After recent careful study of the subject and exploration of the shops, a Chinese connoisseur brought me a piece which he is willing to vouch for as a Sung Kuan, and probably, as judged by the nature of the clay, from the K'ai-fêng kilns. It is a plate or saucer, eight inches in diameter. The colour is an olive green with a very slight tinge of blue. The crackle is finest in the centre, running into larger meshes toward the rim, a considerable portion of the outer edge being uncrackled. The foot is perfectly smooth and finely finished. The piece has rested on a five-pointed object during firing, and the copper-coloured pâte is shown at these five points. It has been buried and shows some iridescence in the bottom, with numerous cloudy spots where the glaze has been eaten away. There is a round black spot in the bottom, which must have been an original defect in the piece. It bears no ornamentation.

Mr. Myers, our consular representative at Mukden, tells me that there is a piece marked "Kuan" in the imperial collection there. He characterises this as of very light sky blue.

HINTS TO THE COLLECTOR

I BELIEVE the search for Sung Kuan a more hopeful one than that for Sung Ju. History indicates that the kilns operated longer, and the list of objects in the T'ao Shuo gives them a much more prominent place. The ware was heavy, and many little objects for the library table, such as seals, were of a form not easily destroyed. They must exist still, both in shops and private collections.

The pâte can hardly be relied on as a distinguishing feature. It was of two varieties, and that of the north must have been very like the Ju and other Honan wares.

It appears always to have been crackled, and there is no record that the crackle was ever of the fish-roe variety. This will serve to distinguish it from the fish-roe crackle Ko wares and from the uncrackled Lung-ch'üan.

There was no cornelian in the glaze, or at least no mention is made of it. The glaze does not appear to have been as thick and unctuous as the Ju.

Made under the imperial eye, as it were, these pieces appear to have been very well finished, but a general air of newness will mark a piece as a Ching-tê-chên imitation.

Colouring matter rubbed into the crackle will help as a means of identification, but it does not appear that this was always done, and the method has been widely used at other kilns.

[104]

THE LUNG-CH'ÜAN CELADONS

IN the specifications for research submitted to me no mention was made of the Lung-ch'üan wares, but the place which they occupy in the history of the Sung potteries is so important that they cannot be omitted without destroying the symmetry of the story. It is not necessary, however, to go into the matter in detail, as there is already a vast amount of literature on the subject, as well as many extant specimens. It is safe to say that the Lung-ch'üan wares are better known, both to foreign collectors and to native connoisseurs, than any other product of the Sung kilns. Dr. Bushell refers to the Lung-ch'üan as "the *ch'ing tz'u*, or green porcelain *par excellence* of the Chinese, the *seiji* of the Japanese, the *martabani* of the Arabs and Persians." In his "Chinese Art," however, he illustrated only two specimens (and these both from the Ming dynasty) of the Lung-ch'üan type, but not from the Lung-ch'üan kilns.

The original Lung-ch'üan potteries were at the villages of Liu-t'ien and Chin-ts'un, at the foot of Liu-hua Shan, in the district of Lung-ch'üan, Ch'u-chou prefecture, province of Chehkiang. The T'ao Lu states that the kilns were in operation from the beginning of the Sung, but whether they began with the Sung or were even older is not stated. They continued to operate until the end of the Yüan dynasty, when they were moved to Ch'u-chou, about seventy-five miles down the river, where work was actively continued until 1620.

A great deal of confusion will be avoided if it be recognised that the Lung-ch'üan celadons did not originate with the Chang brothers. The T'ao Lu discusses them under three heads, the Lung-ch'üan, the Ko, and the Chang Lung-ch'üan, and tells us definitely that the former dated from the *beginning* of the Sung, whereas the others were *during the Sung dynasty*. Dr. Hirth gives the date of the Chang brothers as southern Sung (1127–1278), and on his authority Brinkley refers "the earliest Lung-ch'üan celadons" to this date. This is a misconception. The Chang brothers merely carried on a long-established industry, but made such changes and improvements that from that time their names were attached to the wares. This point is not clearly brought out by all Chinese writers on the subject, and modern Chinese connoisseurs do not seem always to make the distinction. The T'ao Lu is my chief authority for it, but the older works do not refute it, and it seems to me to be brought out in Dr. Hirth's translation from the Ch'ing Pi Tsang, as follows:

"Old Lung-ch'üan porcelain is fine in paste, thick in make, and has an intense onion-green or tree-green colour. The better specimens may compete with the Kuan yao, but there is not much in the way of a crackled surface, a brown paste, and an iron foot. Moreover, they can stand a very great deal of wear and tear and will not easily spoil. But as the manufacturers were somewhat clumsy, the workmanship shown in these porcelains cannot be classed as representing the ancient elegance in style. When the white paste is so covered with green enamel that at the places where it is not put on thick, white patches will shine through, this is the porcelain burned by Chang Sheng of the Sung dynasty, and therefore called Chang yao; when compared to the (ordinary) Lung-ch'üan it displays greater delicacy of workmanship."

Obviously here there is something preceding the Chang yao with which it is compared. The word "ordinary," which Dr. Hirth places in parenthesis, does not occur in the original. If for it we substitute the word "old," actually used at the beginning of the paragraph, we shall see the force of the comparison. It is between the Chang and the older and coarser ware that preceded it, not between the Chang and a contemporary inferior product.

Dr. Hirth also translates from the T'ao Shuo:

"*The Ko yao of the Sung Dynasty.* The porcelain factories of Liu-t'ien were originally in the hands of two brothers," etc. In my opinion, this should read as follows: "*The Ko Kilns of the Sung.* Originally Lung-ch'üan, Liu-t'ien kilns in the hands of two brothers," etc. The text does not require the rendering that these were the first Liu-t'ien kilns, and the context does not support it.

Admitting, then, that there are three sorts of Lung-ch'üan products, and not two, as is usually assumed, let us see what are the characteristics of each.

THE OLD LUNG-CH'ÜAN

ACCORDING to the T'ao Lu, the clay was fine and white. The colour of the glaze was an onion green and there was no crackle. The pieces were heavy and durable and not of very good technique. A kind of basin was made having a pair of fishes on the bottom as decoration and brass rings serving as handles. According to the T'ang Shih Ssu K'ao, only the finest could compete with Kuan and Ko, and few had crackle or the red mouth and iron foot.

THE KO

THIS was ware from the kiln of the elder Chang. The clay was fine and of reddish colour (though perhaps not red until after firing). The fish-roe crackle was so prominent a feature of this ware that the term *Ko yao* has come to be applied in a general way to all monochromes having crackle of this variety. The body was comparatively thin and the colour was a *ch'ing* varying in depth. It does not appear, however, that it was ever an onion green like the older wares, but a native connoisseur tells me that he believes the genuine Ko of the Sung to have been generally of a darker tinge than the Ching-tê-chên imitations. A straw-coloured variety was also produced. Genuine Sung Ko should show the red mouth and iron foot.

THE CHANG LUNG-CH'ÜAN

THESE were from the kilns of the younger brother. They were finer wares than the Old Lung-ch'üan, and differed from the Ko chiefly in having no crackle. Also it is said that some pieces were of "kingfisher" *ch'ing*, a term not used in describing the Ko. It is with regard to the Chang Lung-ch'üan that we are told that, notwithstanding the iron foot, the paste was white where not exposed to the direct heat of the furnace. I incline to the belief that the same is true of the Ko, and that the Chang brothers probably used the same kind of clay. But if we are to accept the statements of the T'ao Lu without reservation, we must hold that the clay of the Old Lung-ch'üan was white before and after firing, that of the Ko reddish, and that of the Chang Lung-ch'üan white with the quality of turning red in the furnace.

With the exception of the notice of a pair of fishes appearing in the bottom of Old Lung-ch'üan basins, the T'ao Lu says nothing with regard to the decoration of Lung-ch'üan wares. We know, however, from existing specimens, that flowers, fishes, scroll-work, etc., similar to the designs used on the Ting yao were commonly applied, both incised and in relief. The Ko relied for decoration on its crackle.

All sorts of articles were made at the Lung-ch'üan kilns. Heavy basins, bowls, and plates seem to have been the characteristic forms of the old ware and of the Chang Lung-ch'üan. The author of the T'ao Shuo enumerates many articles of Ko ware, in quaint and grotesque form, for use on the study table. Many fine vases of the Ko type are now seen, but these are comparatively modern.

VARIETIES AND IMITATIONS

IN addition to the old ware and the work of the Chang brothers, we have seen that similar but somewhat inferior ware was produced at Ch'u-chou until the beginning of the seventeenth century. The Ching-tê-chên kilns have always been active in the imitation of these wares, particularly of the Ko type, and they have turned out products far superior, in workmanship at least, to their originals.

EXAMPLES OF LUNG–CH'ÜAN CELADONS

I AM not aware of having seen any pieces of genuine Sung Ko. I believe, however, that such may be found, particularly in small articles, both in shops and private collections.

A pair of fine vases of the Ko type were recently presented to Mrs. Calhoun by President Yuan Shih-k'ai. These are too fine in workmanship to be referred to the Sung kilns.

I have in my own possession a large plate of the Lung-ch'üan type. It is heavy and of coarse workmanship, sea green in colour, and has a checkered pattern incised in the paste under the glaze. It has the characteristics of the old ware, but may have proceeded from the Ch'u-chou kilns.

Many good celadons are to be found in Japan. In the Baron Iwasaki collection is a spotted celadon dating from the Ming. This *yao pien*, or "furnace transmutation" variety, is exceedingly rare.

Bushell's "Chinese Art" figures two Ming celadons of the Lung-ch'üan type. One of these is a plate with floral decoration incised under the glaze, the other a double-bodied vase, the outer part pierced with scroll foliage.

THE CHŪN

THE Chün wares have never been accorded high rank in Chinese literature. I have followed the order of the T'ao Lu in placing them after the Ting, Ju, Kuan, and Ko; and the T'ao Lu, in doing so, has followed the example of the older writers. The author of the T'ao Shuo describes the ware, quoting various authorities, but I cannot find that he has given it any place in his catalogue of noted pieces. The Chün was not made in the classical shapes of the old bronzes, and its brilliant colouring did not appeal to the old-time Chinese scholars as did the quiet elegance of the Ting and the celadons. They were probably somewhat inclined to class it as they do cloisonné enamels, as "fit only for the apartments of the women and unsuited to the library of a scholar." But intrinsic beauty it always possessed and the passing of years has given it the dignity of the antique. It has fully come into its own, and is enjoying a vogue, both among native and European collectors, which it is not likely to lose. A Chinese friend recently remarked that, from this time onward, a piece of genuine Sung Chün must go on increasing in interest and value, no matter what changes may occur in fads and fashions.

The place at which this ware was made was originally known as Chün-t'ai or Chün-chou, the name being changed to Yü-chou under the Ming dynasty. It is in K'ai-fêng prefecture, province of Honan. Thus the Chün proceeded from the same keramic centre as the early Ch'ai and the Sung Ju and Kuan. The kilns dated "from the beginning of the Sung," so that we may consider the Chün as among the oldest of the Sung wares. Under the Yüan dynasty they turned out the well-known Yüan tz'u, a product inferior to their work under the Sung, but still possessing much merit. When they ceased to operate, I have not been able to learn. The degeneracy of the wares probably began as soon as the Sung capital was transferred to the south.

The T'ao Lu quotes the T'ang Shih Ssu K'ao to the effect that, of the Chün wares, only the pots and saucers for growing the calamus were of really good material. Other articles are said to have been of sandy paste. One finds peculiar discrepancies among writers in English with regard to the quality of the Chün paste. Brinkley calls it a kind of faience, although he speaks of the Ju as a porcelain. This is, of course, a matter of definition of terms. Neither ware approached translucency. Hobson correctly states that the Chün varied from porcellanous stoneware to brown and red pottery. There is no confusion on the subject in the minds of the Chinese. They separate the Chün into two distinct classes, and a dealer or connoisseur will always refer to a piece as *sha t'ai* (sandy paste) or *tz'u t'ai*.[1]

At the beginning of my researches I was very sceptical as to the Sung origin of this latter class. The pâte is very unlike that of other Honan wares, and in comparison with the *sha t'ai* it is found associated with a superior technique which suggests a later and more advanced stage of the art. One naturally suspects that he is confronted with an imitation from the kilns of Ching-tê-chên, but having repeatedly found such pieces vouched for by thoroughly competent and absolutely disinterested Chinese authorities, I now feel compelled to admit their verdict and to credit their explanation. The keeper in charge of the collection of H. E. Sheng Hsüan-huai assured me that during the reign of the Sung emperors a certain amount of tribute clay was annually sent from the vicinity of Ching-tê-chên to be used in the imperial kilns, and that this was devoted to the manufacture of the calamus pots and bowls and other fine articles for imperial use, whereas the coarser articles of *sha t'ai* were made from the native clays. H. E. T'ang Shao-yi corroborates this assertion. Naturally the best quality of glaze and the skill of the best workmen would be applied to the pieces made for imperial use and from tribute clay, and thus we find the great discrepancy in these vases fully accounted for.

The colour and quality of the glazes were the distinguishing features of the Chün. The T'ao Lu says that rouge or cinnabar red was most esteemed, while onion-green and inky-purple ranked next, all three being considered superior provided the colours were pure and unmixed. Other tints produced by the admixture of these three colours in the firing must be regarded as accidents and not separate varieties. If the old potters were really aiming to produce monochromes, examination of existing specimens would indicate that accidents were much more numerous than successful essays.

---

[1] For the discussion of the word *tz'u*, see Glossary; here it means what Hobson calls "porcellanous stoneware."

Among the fanciful names applied to various shades were plum-green, parrot-green, *hai-t'ang* red, pig's liver, mule's lung, mucus, sky-blue, etc. These terms are taken from the books. I have not heard them applied to the Chün wares by native connoisseurs, except in the case of the *t'ien lan*, or "sky-blue." The best reds are referred to as *mei-kuei-hung*, or "rose-red," and *yen-chih*, or "rouge-red." The latter two terms do not mean quite the same tinge, yet I have heard them applied by different connoisseurs to the same piece. Evidently the question of colour terminology is as vexing to the Chinese as to ourselves. I have seen no brilliant greens appearing on genuine Chün, but in streaks and bands where the glaze appears to have run thin one sees a dull tint which I have heard characterised as "eel-skin" or "crab-shell." The old writers lay little stress on the blue shades of this ware, and the pieces in which it prevailed do not appear to have been highly esteemed. Yet, as a matter of fact, blue of varying tint is the prevailing colour in most extant specimens. Like the blue shown in our specimen of Yüan tz'u, it forms a sort of groundwork for the other colours, which appear merely as transmutation effects. In its deeper tint it is *t'ien lan*, or "sky-blue"; when more delicate it approaches *yü ko t'ien ch'ing*, or "blue of the sky after rain." In English works it has been called blue-grey and lavender-grey. It does frequently show a decided tinge of lavender, and it must be remembered that it shades gradually into purple of varying depth, and from purple into the highly prized reds. But even when the outside of the piece approaches nearest to a monochrome red, the lip and lining will still show the blue as a groundwork.

To my mind, there is a strong similarity in colouring running through all the early Honan wares, for which the study of books on the subject, whether native or European, does not fully prepare us. The only place where I have seen the point adequately brought out is in Hobson's introduction to the Catalogue of the Burlington Fine Arts Exhibition of

1910. The old Honan potters were all trying to imitate the Ch'ai, and in their tradition at least the Ch'ai was blue.

That which particularly distinguished the Chün was the furnace transmutation effect. This was probably at first purely accidental and afterward eagerly seized upon and controlled, to some extent at least, by the Chün-chou potters. We have seen the same thing occurring in old celadons, but rarely. As we have noted elsewhere, an unexpected transmutation occurring at Chi-chou so frightened the potters that they closed their kilns and ran away. Fortunately the workmen of Chün-chou were less superstitious.

It should be noted that the Chinese classify furnace transmutation effects as "natural" and "artificial," and that the peculiar excellence of genuine old Chün lies in the fact that it belongs to the former class. The latter I have heard characterised by a Chinese art lover as "hideous." I have seen pieces of Chün described, in catalogues and elsewhere, as though one colour had been applied over another. This could be true only of imitations. Note how in our shards of Yüan tz'u each shade of colour extends through the thick glaze to the body of the piece. A genuine Sung Chün, if broken and examined, will show the same effect.

As a rule, the Chün was not crackled, and this, in my mind, forms one means of distinguishing it from the Yüan dynasty output from the same potteries. The distinction is not absolute, however. There are crackled pieces extant which, owing to the superior quality of their glaze, have been classed as Sung. I have seen one piece uncrackled except for a spot of fine, accidental crackle about the size of a silver dollar on the inside rim.

A passage from the Liu Ch'ing Jih Cha, quoted by the T'ao Lu, speaks of marking called *t'u-ssu wen*, sometimes seen on the Chün wares. This has occasioned much dispute. Julien translates it literally "hare's fur." It is, however, the Chinese name for "dodder," and Dr. Hirth regards this as the more likely rendering. Brinkley, in commenting on the passage

[113]

falls into a peculiar error. He says: "What the passage in
the Liu Ch'ing Jih Cha conveys is that the colours of the
Chün yao presented a variegated appearance, like the green
and white on the leaf of the dodder." This is of course
untenable, as it is a well-known fact that the dodder has no
leaf. However, the yellow stem of the dodder, winding in
and out among the leaves of the plant on which it feeds,
does present a striking colour contrast, and might well be
used for comparison if anything similar occurred in the Chün.
One could easily understand it as applied to the golden lines
seen in the black Chien tea bowls, but the Chün presents no
such appearance, and the term is never heard applied to
Chün by modern Chinese connoisseurs. These latter do,
however, point with great pride to the *ch'iu-ying wen*, or
"earth-worm tracks," which are to be found most clearly
marked in the bottoms of the best pieces. These are the
V-shaped markings to which Brinkley refers as "constituting
in the eyes of some virtuosi the difference between excellence
and mediocrity." They form the only characteristic markings
of the Chün wares, and so far as my observation goes they
are peculiar to the Chün, so that they constitute valuable
marks of genuineness. The more clearly defined they are,
the more highly the piece is prized. To our minds they would
never suggest either "hare's fur" or "dodder," but on the
other hand they do strikingly resemble "earth-worm" tracks,
and that is what the Chinese call them. They are quite
familiar to all who have seen good specimens of Chün saucers
or bulb bowls.

The Chün was undecorated except for the wonderful play
of colours in the glaze, unless the rows of knobs on the outside
of certain pieces be classed as decoration. The wares of the
Chün potters appear to have been for real use rather than
ornament, and this may have tended to discredit them.
The flower pots, with their saucers, on which, as we have seen,
their best skill was expended, were actually adapted to the
purpose of growing plants and not to serve by themselves

as cabinet ornaments. The passage in the T'ao Lu referring to these pots and saucers has proved a stumbling-block to numerous translators, and is itself a fine example of the difficulties with which the Chinese language bristles. Julien, the pioneer, went far afield by rendering it "the vases which had a sword-grass painted on the bottom," while others, recognising the fact that this was never done and endeavouring to correct him, have referred to these pots as characterised by their finely finished bottom. The difficulty is in the Chinese disregard of connectives, and the text is open to almost any construction, even that of Julien. But the experience of the collector conclusively proves that the expression *p'en ti* here used means "the pot *and* its saucer" and not "the bottom of the pot." The pots have holes pierced in the bottom to permit the water to escape, and so necessarily rest in a shallow saucer meant to contain the surplus water. They narrow toward their bases, and the saucers in which they rest should not be wider than the mouths of the pots. There should be similarity of shape—*e.g.*, a hexagonal pot should have a hexagonal saucer. When the two are intact, matching in shape and colouring, the value of each piece is greatly enhanced. Naturally many more saucers than pots are to be found in collections, as from their shape they were much less likely to be destroyed.

There is one variety of dish which I have heard classified by some Chinese collectors as *ti*, or "saucer," and by others as *hsi*, a term usually applied to bowls for washing brushes. Some of these are beautifully finished pieces. Like the ordinary *ti*, they rest upon short legs, but the piece itself is somewhat less shallow than any *ti* which I have seen associated with its *p'en*. These are usually finished with rows of knobs on the outside. Some of them might serve quite satisfactorily as narcissus bulb bowls, and I believe they have been so designated in some European collections. However, I am inclined to think that they originally had pots to match. A friend whose collection I recently had the pleasure of examining had three of these pieces, of varying size and colouring, which he classified as *hsi*. He also possessed a magnificent pot which had lost its saucer. On my expressing regret at the loss of the saucer, he placed each of the three in succession underneath the pot to test the effect. Each had to be rejected, as there was in each case something lacking in size or colouring, but in shape they were perfectly adapted.

Among other articles mentioned in the T'ao Lu as having been manufactured at the Chün kilns are garden stools, small round boxes with covers, square vases and jars.

VARIETIES AND IMITATIONS

It is said that specimens of Chün showing all the variations of colour that we have enumerated were sent from the palace to the Ching-tê-chên factories to serve as models during the reign of Yung Cheng. These would, of course, be the best of their class, and we are told that the imitations were executed with remarkable skill and in great numbers. The T'ao Lu, after citing the criticism of the T'ang Shih Ssu K'ao regarding the coarse sandy material of certain Chün pieces, says: "This can only apply to genuine old Chün, as the Ching-tê-chên imitations showed splendid results in vases and jars also." Evidently the author means to assert that in the case of vases, jars, etc., at least so far as the quality of the paste is concerned, the imitation is to be distinguished from the original by its superiority. We must remember, however, that this author was writing the history of the Ching-tê-chên kilns, not the history of pottery in general, and that he was interested in glorifying the work of the Ching-tê-chên potter. The modern Chinese connoisseur prizes a good Yung Cheng Chün as a thing of interest and beauty in itself, but he classes it far below his genuine old Chün, and so far as I can judge from the specimens examined, there is no reason why he should ever mistake the one for the other.

But the kilns of Ching-tê-chên have been turning out

imitations of the Chün wares since the Yung Cheng period, and I understand that the Japanese have done the same. There was nothing fraudulent in the work of the Yung Cheng potter. He was honestly striving to emulate, and if possible to improve upon, the old art. But, according to Burton, these later imitators are working with intent to deceive. He says that their works are clever forgeries, and that they imitate so well the technical imperfections of the old wares that it seems impossible to distinguish them. The Chün wares of *sha t'ai*, or sandy paste, have been imitated in I-hsing clay.

The Yüan tz'u, which is the Yüan dynasty descendant of the Sung Chün, and which in native collections is usually found side by side with it though far less highly prized, deserves a section to itself.

EXAMPLES OF THE CHÜN WARES

In the opinion of H. E. T'ang Shao-yi, the best complete set of Chün pieces now in existence consists of four flower pots, with their saucers intact, eight pieces in all, which were formerly the property of Her Majesty the late Empress Dowager Tzu Hsi. These were so highly prized by her that she kept them always upon the table before her throne or chair of state, filled with flowers appropriate to the season, and there Mr. T'ang several times had the opportunity of seeing them. These pots are hexagonal in shape, and the colour is the finest vermilion. Mr. T'ang never had the opportunity of examining them closely, and could not describe them in detail, but in his judgment they are priceless. He believes them to be still stored in the palace, though it is conceivable that during the troublous period of the Dynasty's downfall they may have been stolen and concealed, or even put upon the market by eunuchs or palace servants.

The finest collection of Chün to which I have been given access is that of Mr. (Chao) Ch'ing K'uan, a retired Manchu gentleman resident in Peking.[1] Among his pieces I may mention the following:

A well-matched flower pot and saucer, each quadrangular in shape, the pot widening toward the top, as most of these pieces do, and presenting the appearance of a truncated pyramid inverted. The blue of the groundwork is the *t'ien-lan*, or sky-blue, and the prevailing colour is a fine red. This red being the colour most highly prized by the Chinese, Mr. Ch'ing K'uan considers the set the best in his collection. The incised numeral is 10.

Another set—pot and saucer—are oblong hexagonal. The prevailing colour is a splendid *aubergine*. This pot is remarkable for its "earth-worm tracks," which are peculiarly noticeable both outside and inside. Inside they are largely V-shaped markings, but outside they extend in long lines which really resemble more than any others that I have seen the lines which might be made by an earth-worm wriggling in the sand. Unfortunately the rim of this pot had been removed owing to injury, and the exposed upper portion of the pot had been ground down and painted brown. The numeral of the pot is 7, and that of the saucer 10.

Another set has four rounded sides and shows an *aubergine* colouring somewhat lighter than the preceding. Its "earth-worm tracks" are also less striking. The pot is number 4, and the saucer 8.

I did not measure any of these pieces. The height of the pots as they rested in the saucers probably average about seven inches. Both pots and saucers rest upon squat feet corresponding in number to the sides. The bottoms of the pots are pierced with holes to permit the escape of surplus water. They also show numerous small spur-marks.

There is one pot with globular body and spreading mouth, but without saucer. This is about seven inches high. The prevailing colour is blue, but some good touches of red appear on the bulging portion outside. The numeral is 6.

[1] The surname *Chao* has been assumed by Mr. Ch'ing K'uan since the revolution made him a Chinese citizen.

This collection also contains a number of fine *hsi*, or bowls for washing brushes. It was by this term that the owner invariably referred to them. However, hereafter I shall mention such pieces as "bulb bowls," that being the name usually given them by writers in English.[1]

I was not able to see the collection of H. E. T'ang Shao-yi, it being stored in Tientsin. He showed me, however, one favourite piece kept in his home in Shanghai. This is a bulb bowl about three inches high and six inches in its greatest diameter. The best colouring is the purple of the upper inside part. The bottom of the interior is dotted and mottled and of a nondescript colour which Mr. T'ang characterised as "onion *ch'ing*," explaining, however, that in his idea the *ch'ing* of the onion is more blue than green. The great beauty of the piece is in the excellence of its V-shaped markings or "earth-worm tracks," which are peculiarly well defined. The exterior is finished with the usual row of knobs. The numeral is 9.

The best specimens of Sung Chün in the collection of H. E. Sheng Hsüan-huai were destroyed by a shell during the recent fighting at the Kiangnan Arsenal. Among the articles remaining were:

A flower pot which the keeper characterised as a Sung Chün but not a Kuan or Imperial Chün. It is of *sha t'ai*, or sandy paste.

A *ti*, or saucer, about three inches in its greatest diameter, the upper rim incurved. This is of crude appearance but has some good spots of red colouring. A mass of glaze is collected at the bottom. The piece may be regarded as an accident of the furnace, and, though not well finished, is interesting.

A writer's small water pot of *tz'u t'ai*, or the better quality of paste. The colour is "blue of the sky after rain" and the glaze remarkably thick, as may be seen where it is collected in irregular masses at the base.

[1] Mr. Ch'ing K'uan's excellent collection of Yüan *tz'u* will be mentioned elsewhere.

[119]

A large plate of *sha t'ai*, the colour purple and blue with lines of red.

A bowl with crackle and the colour effects showing in large splashes. This had to me the appearance of Yüan tz'u, but the keeper said that he classified it as Sung owing to the peculiar lustre of the glaze.

In a shop off Kiukiang Road, Shanghai, I found an excellent specimen of *hsi*, or bulb bowl. It is a little over three inches high, and more than nine inches in diameter. The colours are sky-blue and *aubergine*, and the V-shaped markings are excellent. On a spot inside, about the size of a silver dollar, a fine crackle appears. The numeral is 2. The dealer informed me that this piece belonged to a private collection and had been placed with him to be sold on commission.

In the Wen Yüan Tzü, Newchwang Road, Shanghai, I found a piece called by the dealer a flower pot, which might be described as beaker-shaped. It has a bulging centre, narrowing abruptly and then widening again to the foot. The original shape of the upper portion could not be determined, as it had been injured and a portion ground off. A part of the upper portion still appears, but the symmetry is destroyed. The prevailing colour was called by the dealer *mei-kuei-hung*, or "rose-red," but to my eye this red bears a distinct tinge of purple. The groundwork and inner lining are sky-blue, and a colour something like eel-green appears at the edges where the glaze has run thin. A splash of blue colour appears on the inverted bottom. Four bars project from each of the three sections of the piece. The numeral is 6.[1]

Mr. Chun Chik-yu writes me that he possesses three first-class specimens of genuine "Northern Sung Chün," and he figures and describes a pot with its saucer. These two pieces have four rounded sections and are oblong in shape, the greatest length being seven inches and the greatest width five and

---

[1] H. E. T'ang Shao-yi and H. E. Chang Yin-t'ang both examined this piece and certified to its genuineness, though they considered its value greatly deteriorated by the injury to the upper portion. The colouring they pronounced extremely good.

a fraction. The pot is two and three-eighths inches high. The paste he calls a "white, warm wax colour," and says that this may be determined by examination where the glaze has run thin, and also by the spur-marks. It is "hard, compact, and lustrous," qualities which give a good background for the glaze. The colour is a deep plum-purple with touches of rose-red at the four legs. A yellowish wax colour shows at the edges, and the inside is bluish. "Both inside and outside are covered with a thin frost, and the worm markings show the truer colours." Mr. Chun encloses a drawing of the "earth-worm markings." Like the piece described from the collection of Mr. Ch'ing K'uan, these are V-shaped on the inside of the piece, and outside run into longer lines, which really suggest the name given them. A few fine crackles which Mr. Chun calls "age-crackles" are to be found "in the parts exposed to water." The bottom shows five colours—dark rose-red, dark purple, sky-blue, yellowish olive, and, at the numeral mark and another spot where the glaze is thin, a tobacco brown. The numeral is 7.[1]

An interesting collection examined is that of Mr. Kuan Mien-chün of Peking. In addition to various pieces similar to those already described, he has a garden stool about two feet high, similar in size and shape to those manufactured and used nowadays, which he believes to be a genuine Sung Chün. As one would expect from the reference to these stools in the T'ao Lu, it is of *sha t'ai*, and not the finest technique, but it is none the less an object of great beauty and interest. It has openings in the shape of animal heads called *shou t'ou*, and is decorated with rows of knobs. The prevailing colour is "blue of the sky after rain," but is quite flecked and dappled. The glaze is pitted in places with tiny holes which Mr. Kuan called "ant-tracks." On the unglazed surface of the interior are peculiar markings which look as though the paste had been

---

[1] In many pieces examined I have noted the frosty appearance to which Mr. Chun refers. The colour, particularly on the inside, which is usually blue, is deeper and clearer where the V-shaped marks occur.

pressed and patted into shape with a shell. The stool was excavated along the line of the Pien-Loh Railway. I had the temerity to ask Mr. Kuan its value. He said that it cost him "three obeisances," and was not for sale at any price.

Among Mr. Kuan's specimens was a flower pot from the kilns of Ching-tĕ-chĕn. It was not meant to deceive, for it bore the Yung Cheng mark. The colour is too uniform as compared with the old pieces, and the glaze lacks the peculiar opalescent quality of the Sung Chün. The technique is excellent.

This list is already so long that I will not describe the various pieces noted in catalogues, etc. I would, however, call the attention of the reader to the Catalogue of the Burlington Fine Arts Exhibition of 1910.

HINTS TO THE COLLECTOR

THE Chün kilns operated for a long time, and the output was probably large. The wares were heavy and durable, therefore it is reasonable to suppose that genuine pieces have survived to the present day.

The paste is of two sorts—a light-coloured, hard, compact paste called *tz'u t'ai*, and a dark, sandy paste called *sha t'ai*. Genuine pieces of the former will be found chiefly in the shape of flower pots and bowls; of the latter, in vases, various small objects for the study, etc.

The quality of the glaze can be learned by experience only, not by description. Perhaps the word which best describes it is "opalescent."

Red is the colour most highly prized. *Aubergine*-purple ranks second. Pieces in which either of these colours prevails are very highly prized. Even slight flecks or streaks of the red give a piece value.

The "earth-worm tracks" are found on all the best pieces.

Chün ware is usually not crackled. If crackle does exist, it is incidental, and, if I understand Mr. Chun's theory, not due to the cracking of the paste in cooling, but to age and contact with water.

All really good specimens have the incised numeral underneath. It is, of course, understood that the numeral in itself proves nothing.

Hobson, in his preface to the Catalogue of the Burlington Fine Arts Exhibition, speaks of a reddish-brown dressing which appears on the bottom of some of the pieces classified in that collection as Sung Chün. He remarks that but for the trustworthy evidence of Chinese connoisseurs to the contrary, this dressing would lead him to consider the articles Yung Cheng imitations. My experience has been the same. Some of the best pieces that I have seen have this dressing, yet they are owned by men who have spent a lifetime and practically unlimited funds in making their collections. If they have been deceived, how shall we escape! But personally I should prefer a bottom with glaze of variegated colouring like that described by Mr. Chun. I have seen no statement in literature as to how the old Chün potters finished the bottoms of their pieces.

The market is flooded with imitations in response to the present-day popular demand. I make this statement on the authority of William Burton, F.C.S. ("Porcelain: a Sketch of its Nature, Art, and Manufacture"). In his opinion, some of the later imitations, Chinese and Japanese, can hardly be distinguished from the originals.

Nevertheless, it is not the art shops of Peking or Shanghai that are so flooded, for the casual customer rarely sees a piece that even claims to be Sung Chün. When such a piece is in the possession of a dealer, it is produced only when asked for, and is usually brought forth from some back room or upper chamber, where it has been hidden.

Prices are high and mounting. The value of a flower pot or bulb bowl of good colour and marking runs into thousands. These values, now established, are not likely to decrease, unless absolutely successful imitations are made in large numbers.

[123]

THE CHIEN

CHINESE writers do not class this ware among the important products of the Sung dynasty. As it was not imitated at the Ching-tê-chên kilns, the T'ao Lu discusses it only in the chapter on "Ancient Wares," and gives a brief description which appears to be quoted from the Ko Ku Yao Lun. The T'ao Shuo, however, devotes some space to an account of the vogue which this ware enjoyed among the tea clubs of ancient times. Chinese connoisseurs of the present day know very little about it, but the Japanese appear to be full of enthusiasm on the subject.

This ware was made during the Sung dynasty, in what is now the district of Chien-yang, Chien-ning prefecture, province of Fukien. The city was at that time called Chien-chou. According to the T'ao Lu, the kilns continued to flourish during the Yüan dynasty.

The Ko Ku Yao Lun says that the pieces were, as a rule, quite heavy. Such lighter pieces as were produced were worthy to rank with other good Sung productions. The heavy cups were much sought after by the tea-drinkers, however, as they had the quality of retaining heat. The Ts'ai Hsiang Ch'a Lu says that in this respect the Chien bowls excelled the products of all other districts, and that the celadons and the white wares were never used in the "tea contests."

The famous glaze of the Chien must not be conceived as a black monochrome. It was a background of black with blue and purple iridescences and shot through with lines of golden brown. It is these lines which are compared to "hare's fur," and which may be regarded as one of the chief distinguishing marks of the Chien ware. The Ko Ku Yao Lun also mentions "pearl drops" which appear on the Chien bowls. It is not clear whether these are yellow marks which appear in round, pearl-like spots instead of lines, or whether they are patches similar to the "tear-drops" of the Ting.

A book called the Ch'ing I Lu calls the lines on the Chien

ware "partridge markings." This appears to refer to a dappled rather than streaked appearance.

In the specifications submitted to me mention was made of certain decorative designs in the Chien ware, such as "birds in reserve," which were sometimes left in the bare paste, and also "designs of night and day," "running water effects," "still pools," and other interesting suggestive designs, such as "rabbit's fur." It is quite possible that designs in reserve were sometimes left in the Chien cups, as was occasionally done in the Lung-ch'üan ware, but I have seen no mention of such a practice in either European or Chinese literature. Brinkley says that sometimes, in specimens of later date, the decoration takes the form of conventional phœnixes, butterflies, maple leaves, etc., "in golden brown of the most satisfying richness and beauty." I find in Chinese literature no evidence that there was ever any intentional designing on the old Fukien tea bowls. A Japanese lady, in explaining to me the peculiar esteem in which these bowls have always been held by the people of her country, said that they were able to see in them "all sorts of scenery," but she did not mean that scenic effects had been definitely traced and intentionally produced.

The vogue enjoyed by the Chien wares among tea-drinkers was in part due to the thickness of the material, but this was a quality which might be easily attained at any kiln. The colour of the glaze was a far more important factor in its popularity. Tea-drinking in ancient times was a cult—a ceremonial observance—with which the cultured taste of the day wished to associate all pleasure possible. The blending of the *Chien yao* glazes with the colours of the tea was considered to give the most pleasing nuance of colour that the potter's art had achieved. This glaze was also considered to have the power of preventing, or rather retarding, the process of evaporation, and for this reason the wares were sometimes called "the slow-drying cups." To understand the Chinese appreciation of this quality one must know that the "tea contest" was merely a process of matching cups owned by different individuals to determine whose cup would retain moisture longest. He whose cup was able to show a trace of moisture after the others were entirely dry was the winner of the tournament. This appears to have been as exciting to the old-time Chinese as is the Derby to a modern Englishman. The T'ao Shuo calls attention to the fact that the sharp contrast of colour between the tea and the black glaze facilitated the task of the umpire.

I am not prepared to give the history of the Chien tea bowl in Japan. It appears to have been much more appreciated there than in China, as its very crudeness made it appropriate to the tea ceremonial, a very different process from the Chinese tea contest. It appears that a large portion of the Chien output found its way to Japan, and also that reproductions and modifications of the ware have been produced in great quantities, both in Japan and Corea.

Various small articles other than tea bowls were doubtless produced at the Chien kilns; but, considered as a keramic product simply, the ware was very lightly esteemed and few such articles have been preserved.

VARIETIES AND IMITATIONS

THE T'ao Shuo, in its discussion of the Chien wares, quotes one authority to the effect that the black "hare's-fur" cups for the tea contests were first made at Ting-chou. We have seen elsewhere that the Ting-chou kilns did produce a black ware.

The *wu-ni yao*, or "raven-clay ware," appears to have been an inferior, and, judging by the arrangement of the T'ao Lu, an earlier product of the same factories. As the name shows, the clay was very dark. It was sometimes given a celadon glaze, and the P'ing Hua P'u compares it favourably with the Lung-ch'üan products, whereas other authorities dismiss it as unworthy of discussion.

EXAMPLES OF THE CHIEN WARE

I HAVE not been able to find any cups classified as Chien in Peking shops or private collections. The collection of Mr. Ch'ing K'uan contains a wide-mouthed bowl with dark brown glaze, dappled with lighter brown, which might be considered as corresponding to the descriptions given. The owner believes it to be a Sung, but says that it is not from the Chien kilns. It may be a Ting-chou product.

In the Burlington Fine Arts Exhibition of 1910 were shown two Chien bowls classified as Sung or Yüan. They were the property of Mr. W. A. Alexander. They are of dark brown stoneware with thick, purplish black glaze shot with golden brown. The rims are protected (or concealed) with metal bands.

A small vase in the same exhibition was classed as probably Chien. It was described as follows: "Vase of oval form with straight neck, wide mouth, and two loop handles; pale buff stoneware, thin brown glaze inside; in neck and on outside thick glaze of purplish black streaked and mottled with golden brown,[1] stopping in an uneven line short of the base. Height, four and three-fourths inches. Property of R. H. Benson."

We are told that numerous excellent specimens of this ware are to be found in Japan, and it had best be studied from that standpoint. It will be necessary, however, to discriminate carefully between real Sung Chien and similar Japanese and Corean pieces.

MINOR KILNS OF THE SUNG

THE TZ'U-CHOU KILNS

THESE have already been mentioned in connection with Ting wares. Tz'u-chou anciently formed part of Chang-te Fu in Honan, but is now under the jurisdiction of Kuang-

---

[1] The dappled appearance of the golden brown in the illustration might suggest "partridge feathers" or "pearls."

p'ing in Chihli. It is to the south of Ting-chou. The T'ao Lu tells us that the wares made there were as fine as Ting, but never had the tear-marks. There were both incised and painted styles of decoration. The latter was usually in brown, and there are many extant specimens of the heavy *t'u Ting* type bearing this brown decoration. Many fine pieces from the collection of Mr. G. Eumorfopoulus were shown in the Burlington Fine Arts Exhibition of 1910. Prominent among these are figures of Shou Lao, and other images.

We have seen that brown decoration was sometimes used on the Ting, but it was so much more common in the Tz'u-chou ware that this is by far the safer classification for such a piece. The distinction is unimportant, for the wares were so alike that Chinese authorities admit the impossibility of distinguishing them.

Sometimes the entire piece was glazed and painted brown and then a portion etched away, leaving the design showing in the bare paste. Examples of this sort are not uncommon in the shops. They occur most frequently in the form of large jars.

The Tz'u-chou kilns have never ceased to operate. They are still turning out a cheap ware, commonly used in Peking for domestic purposes and quite similar in style and decoration to the highly prized wares of ancient times.

THE TUNG KILNS

THESE were private kilns which operated near K'ai-fêng Fu when that city was the capital of the Northern Sung. They produced a celadon somewhat similar to that of the imperial kilns, but of inferior quality. They showed the "red mouth and iron foot" so much prized by connoisseurs, and had no crackle. The uninitiated might find some difficulty in distinguishing them from the uncrackled Lung-ch'üan celadons.

The Chinese ideograph for *Tung* originally applied to these wares was that meaning "east." Owing to identity of sound, it has in the course of time become altered to the ideograph which means "winter," so that the term may now be rendered "winter-green." Under this latter term a number of specimens are catalogued in the T'ao Shuo.

THE TENG KILNS

THESE were at Teng-chou in Nan-yang prefecture, province of Honan. They produced a ware somewhat resembling the Ju.

THE YAO KILNS

YAO-CHOU was under the prefecture of Hsi-an in Shensi. These kilns produced a ware resembling the Ju, but inferior, and also a white ware.

THE YŪ-HANG KILNS

THESE were at Yü-hang hsien, Hang-chou prefecture, province of Chehkiang. The colour of the ware was like that of the Kuan, but it lacked gloss. It was uncrackled.

THE LI-SHUI KILNS

AT Li-shui hsien, Ch'u-chou prefecture, province of Chehkiang. Their product was an inferior celadon somewhat resembling the Lung-ch'üan.

THE HSIAO KILNS

THESE were at Hsiao hsien, Hsü-chou prefecture, province of Kiangsu. Here also was the "Village of White Clay," and the kilns were sometimes called the "White Clay Kilns." The product was a rather fine white ware.

THE CHI-CHOU KILNS

THESE were the somewhat noted kilns of what is now Chi-an Fu in the province of Kiangsi. There are said to have been five different manufactories there, of which those of a Mr. Shu and his daughter Shu Chiao were the best known. They made white and purple wares, the latter resembling the purple Ting.

An interesting tradition connected with these kilns is that on one occasion a certain high official paid them a visit, whereupon, presumably in his honour, a batch of vessels then in the oven were suddenly transformed into jade. One would suppose that this might have been regarded as an excellent omen; but, on the contrary, we are told that the potters were so frightened that they closed their kilns and ran away to Jao-chou to take up work there in the Ching-tê-chên factories. This story is supposed to have had its origin in some unusual and unexpected transmutation effects.

THE HSIANG KILNS

THE location of these is not known with certainty, but they are said to have been in Hsiang-shan hsien, in Ningpo prefecture. They operated under the Southern Sung and produced a white ware with crab's-claw crackle, the finer pieces of which were compared with Ting.

THE YÜ-TZ'U KILNS

THESE were at Yü-tz'u hsien, Tai-yüan Fu, province of Shansi. They continued a manufacture which had been begun under the T'ang dynasty, and produced a coarse, heavy ware.

THE P'ING-YANG KILNS

THESE were also in Shansi and continued a work begun under the T'ang. These two Shansi kilns are of no interest except for the primitive character of their work. It being very heavy and durable, specimens doubtless exist to the present day.

THE SU-CHOU KILNS

LOCATED at what is now Fêng-yang Fu, they made an imitation of the Ting which was quite widely disseminated.

KERAMIC WARES OF THE SUNG DYNASTY

THE SZE-CHOU KILNS

THESE were in the province of Anhui. The ware was also in imitation of the Ting.

NOTE. With so many kilns turning out white wares of the Ting type and celadons of varying shades, all heavy and durable in character, one cannot help suspecting that many extant specimens classed as Ting, Kuan, Ju, etc., if really dating from the Sung, are products of the minor kilns. Particularly is this true of the many pieces which lack the finish and the beauty which a study of the literature of the famous kilns has led us to anticipate.

WARES OF THE YŪAN DYNASTY

UNDER the Yüan rulers there was no sudden change in the keramic art, but the product gradually deteriorated owing to lack of imperial patronage. It is, of course, often impossible now to determine with certainty to which period many pieces belong, and the classification "Sung or Yüan" is often the only safe one to adopt. Native connoisseurs seem to be guided chiefly by the quality of the glaze in deciding the question, and in many cases admit their inability to decide.

White wares of the Ting type continued to be made, the nearest approach to the excellence of the genuine northern Ting probably being the work of P'eng Chün-pao of Ho-chou. The Ching-tê-chên kilns turned out white wares and celadons, and it is said that the pieces destined for the court were marked with the characters "Shu Fu." We have seen that the Lung-ch'üan kilns were still active, but their work was of inferior quality.

But though white wares and celadons were made under the Yüan dynasty, the term *Yüan tz'u* as used by the Chinese to-day almost invariably means the somewhat degenerate output of the Chün kilns, shards of which are shown in our exhibition. Along with the superior Sung Chün, this ware is enjoying a great vogue among collectors to-day. Many broken pieces may be seen in the Peking shops, and they are frequently ground into various shapes for belt buckles and other ornaments. Pieces in good condition are also not uncommon, and those showing good colouring command a high price. The colouring is similar to that of the Chün, but, as elsewhere noted, the transmutation tints are more likely to appear in bold splashes of colour, rather than in streaked and dappled effects. Crackle is far more common, and the paste is not so good as in the best quality of Chün. However, the Chinese, in deciding, seem to be guided chiefly by the quality of the glaze. A crackled piece with bold spots of colouring, which I should have unhesitatingly pronounced Yüan, was classed by its owner as Sung Chün owing to the rich, opalescent character of the glaze, which he said never was achieved during the Yüan period.

Fine bowls and plates of this ware may be seen in Peking, both in shops and private collections. In the collection of Mr. Ch'ing K'uan, for example, may be seen a magnificent tripod censer over a foot high, with cover. The upper rim, having sustained injury, has been ground down and finished with a band of copper, and ornaments in the shape of deer's heads have been added. Another similar censer, somewhat smaller, has rim and ears intact, and is ornamented with a dragon in relief. Both show splendid colouring. Mr. Ch'ing K'uan also has eight small bowls showing good spots of colour, and so well matched that one feels almost inclined to question their antiquity. Among various other articles, he called my attention to a gourd-shaped vase, the top ending in seven tubes, each with separate opening to contain a single flower, and finished at the neck with a decoration simulating a knotted ribbon. To him the peculiar excellence of this piece lies in a single tricoloured spot which shows red, purple, and a greenish turquoise in concentric circles—a most interesting trick of the furnace.

ROSE SICKLER WILLIAMS.

[133]

GLOSSARY OF CHINESE
TERMS

GLOSSARY OF CHINESE TERMS

Yao (窯). This ideograph is derived from the radical *hsüeh* (穴), meaning a cave or pit, and the phonetic *kao* (羔). A kiln; the product of a kiln; pottery in its widest sense.

Yao chiang (窯匠). A potter.

Yao kung (窯工). Potter's work.

Yao (窰). Another form of the foregoing, derived from the radical "cave" and *yao* (缶), a jar. The first form is the more correct.

T'ao (陶): from the radical *fu*, a mound, and the phonetic *t'ao* (匋), which latter is also used without the radical and having the same meaning. A kiln.

T'ao jen. A potter.

T'ao ch'i. Pottery.

(Though *yao* and *t'ao* may be alike defined "kiln," the usage is not the same. *T'ao* is never used to designate the wares emanating from the kilns unless it has the word *ch'i*, "wares," following it.)

Ting yao (定窯). Wares of Ting-chou; subsequent wares of the Ting type.

Pei Ting (北定). Northern Ting.

Pai Ting (白定). White Ting.

Nan Ting (南定). Southern Ting.

Fen Ting (粉定). Said by the T'ao Lu to be applied to the same ware as the term *pai Ting*.

T'u Ting (土定). Literally, "earth Ting": a coarse, crackled Ting.

Ju yao (汝窯). Wares of Ju-chou.

Kuan yao (官窯). Imperial ware; modern application, the wares made for imperial use at the Ching-tê-chên kilns.

Sung Kuan yao (宋官窯). Imperial ware of the Sung: specifically applied to the product of the kilns which were located at the capital, but not restricted to these in colloquial use.

[137]

Ko yao (哥窑). Literally, "elder-brother" ware; the ware made at Lung-ch'üan by the elder Chang: commonly applied to other wares having the fine fish-roe crackle of the Sung Ko.

Lung-ch'üan yao (龍泉窑). Wares made at Lung-ch'üan.

Chang Lung-ch'üan (章龍泉). The wares made by the younger Chang.

Chün yao (鈞窑). The wares made at Chün-t'ai, now Yü-chou.

Chien yao (建窑). Wares of Fukien province: modernly applied to the ivory-white, or blanc-de-Chine.

Sung Chien yao (宋建窑). The black or dark-coloured ware made in Fukien under the Sung.

Ch'ai yao (柴窑). A ware made at Cheng-chou previous to the Sung. Largely traditional: supplied the type for the Honan wares of the Sung.

Pi-sê yao (秘色窑). "Secret colour" ware; a ware of a colour reserved for imperial use.

Sui-ch'i yao (碎器窑). Crackled ware: specifically applied to a ware made at Chi-chou which had a colouring pigment rubbed into the crackle.

Wa (瓦). A brick; a tile: commonly used to distinguish earthenware from stoneware and porcelain.

Han wa (漢瓦). Earthenware of the Han period: commonly used to designate Han tiles and all recent finds of mortuary pottery which do not rise to the rank of stoneware.

Tz'u (瓷): from the radical *wa* (瓦) and the phonetic *tz'u* (次). Defined in the Shuo Wen, the oldest Chinese dictionary, as "*wa ch'i*," or "earthenware." Defined in the Lei Pien, a dictionary of the Sung period, as "the harder and finer product of the kilns." Commonly applied now to stoneware and porcelain.

Tz'u (磁): from the radical *shih* (石), a stone, and the phonetic *tz'u* (兹). Sometimes incorrectly used for the foregoing. Defined in the Shuo Wen as "a stone that attracts iron"; a loadstone. Also the name of the *Chou* city in south Chihli where wares were produced similar to the Ting type. From the fact that this city produced such wares, and that the sound is identical with that of the word meaning "stoneware or porcelain," a certain confusion in the use of the word has arisen. But there is no such confusion in the mind of the Chinese scholar. The purist never uses it; and all arguments as to the date of the origin of porcelain which have been based on the use of this word are valueless.

T'ai (胎). Literally, "the womb"; a framework; as applied to porcelain, the body or paste.

Sha t'ai (沙胎). A sandy paste.

Tz'u t'ai (瓷胎). A stoneware or porcelain paste.

GLOSSARY

T'o t'ai (脫胎). Wares from which the body has been removed; egg-shell wares. The Chinese also speak of "semi *t'o t'ai*." I should regard the introduction of these terms as marking the date of the advent of true porcelain in the sense of a translucent ware.

Yu (釉). The glaze. The T'ao Lu calls attention to the fact that this character is frequently written in various incorrect forms.

Wen (紋). Lines or markings.

Sui wen (碎紋). Crackle.

Yü-tz'u wen (魚子紋). Fish-roe crackle.

Hsieh-chua wen (蟹爪紋). Crab's-claw crackle.

Ch'iu-ying wen (蚯蚓). Earth-worm tracks: the characteristic markings of the best Chün. (This is a common colloquial term not found in literature.)

T'u-ssu wen (兔絲紋). Dodder markings (?).

Huang-t'u pan (黄兔斑). Hare's-fur markings: applied to the black Chien.

Kao-lin (高嶺). Literally, "a high range": applied to the hills near Ching-tê-chên from which the clay so called was first derived.

Pe-tun tz'u (白墩子). "White briquettes"; the porcelain stone after having been pulverized and shaped into bricks.

Ch'ing (青). Green, blue, black, or grey. (See note to translation.)

Yü ko t'ien ch'ing (雨過天青). "Blue of the sky after rain": colour of the traditional Ch'ai. Said by modern connoisseurs to be a delicate grey-blue.

Fen ch'ing (粉青). A pale *ch'ing*.

Mei-tz'u ch'ing (梅子青). Plum-green.

T'ien-lan (天藍). Sky-blue.

Yüeh-pai (月白). Moon-white.

Chu-hung (硃紅). Vermilion red.

Chu-sha hung (硃砂紅). Cinnabar red.

Mei-kuei hung (玫瑰紅). Rose-red.

Mei-kuei tz'u (玫瑰紫). A purplish red.

Ch'ieh-p'i tz'u (茄皮紫). Aubergine, or "egg-plant" purple.

The above are appended in the belief that they may be of interest, particularly to the student who has some knowledge of the Chinese characters.

ILLUSTRATIONS

The comparative sizes of the illustrations do not correspond with the comparative sizes of the objects themselves. In each case the dimensions will be found under the description in the catalogue.

1

2

3

4

5

6

7

8

9

10

12

II

13

14

15

16

17

18

19

20

21

22

23

24   25

26   27

28

30

29

31

32   33

36 and 37

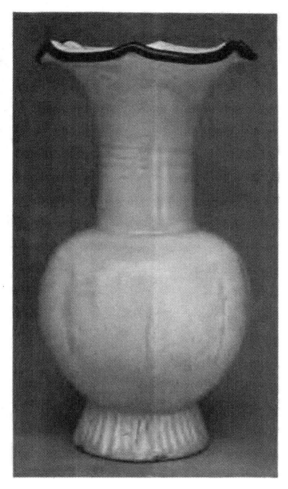

34

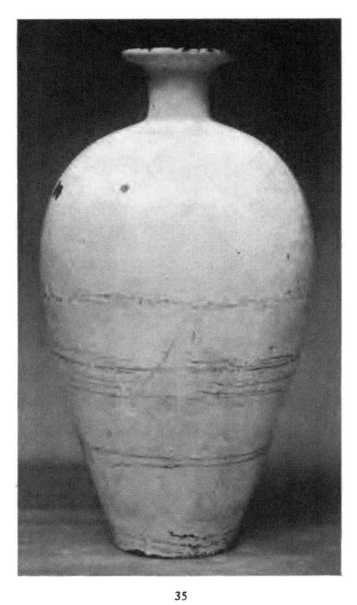

35

38

39

40

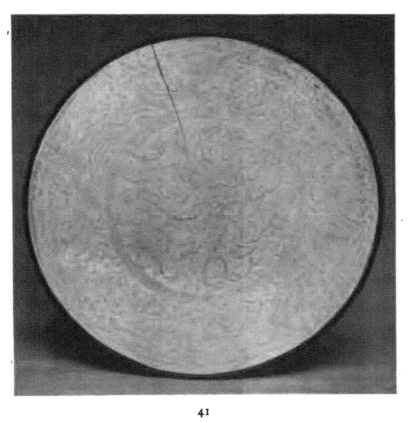

41

42

45

43

47

44

46

48

50

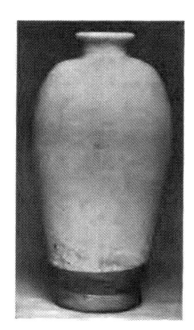

51

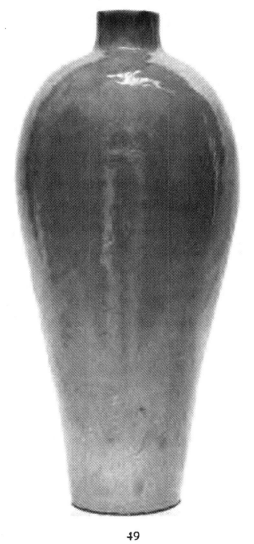

49

52

54

53

55

56

57

58

59

60

61

62

63 and 64

65

66

67

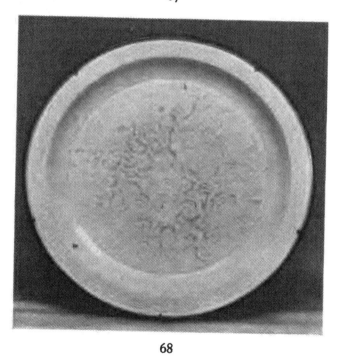

68

69

70

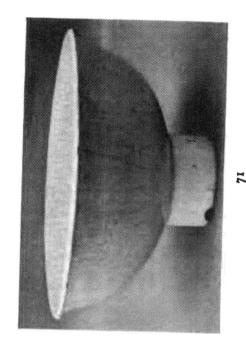

71

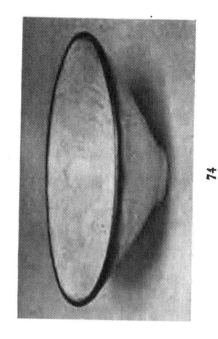

74

73

72

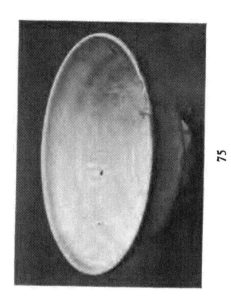

75

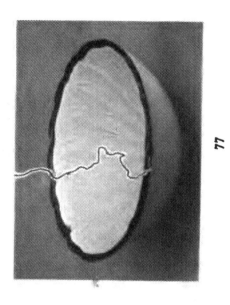

77

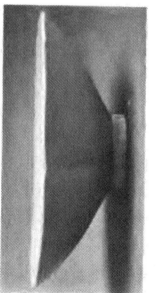

76

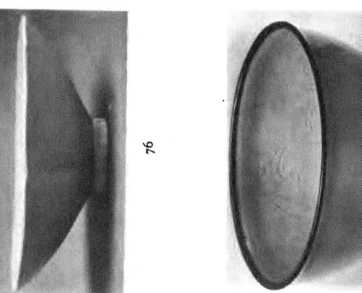

78

79

81 and 82

83

84

85

80

86

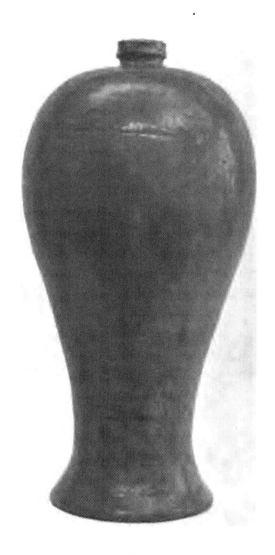

87

88

89

90

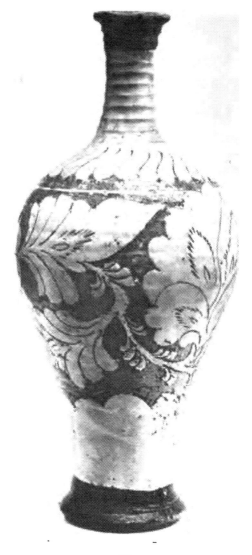

91

92

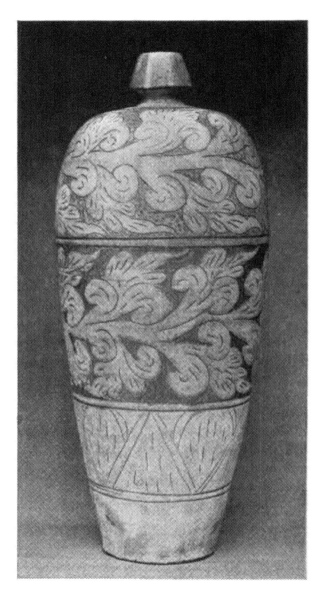

93

94

99

97

95

96

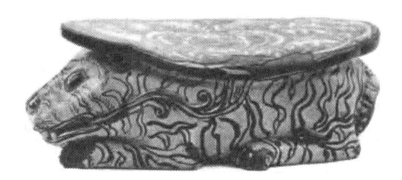

98

100

101

102

103

104

105

106

107

108

109

112

111

119

110

113 and 114

115 and 116

117   118

120

121

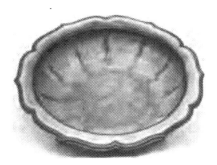

123

122

125

124

126

127

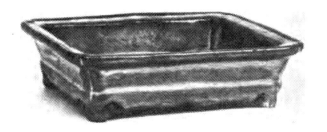

128

129

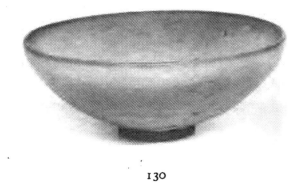

130

131

132

133

134   135

136

141

137

142

139

138

140

143

144

145

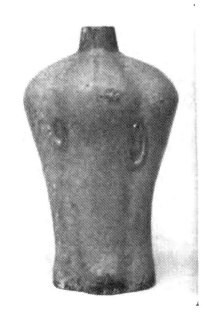

146

147

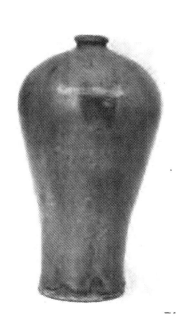

148   149

150

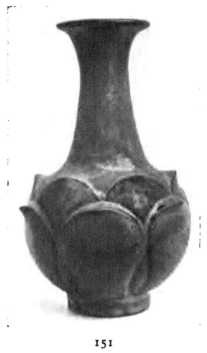

151

152

153

155

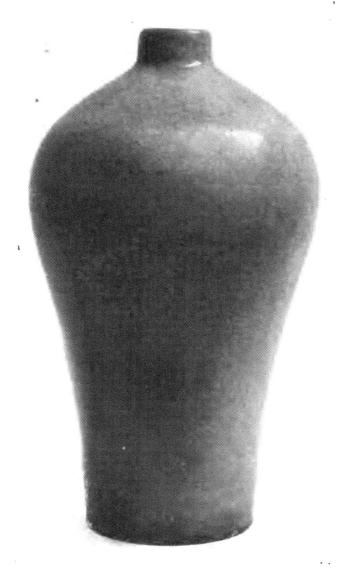

154

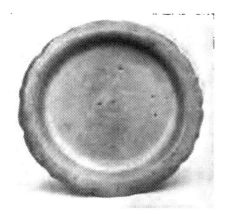

156 157

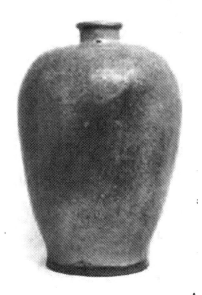

158

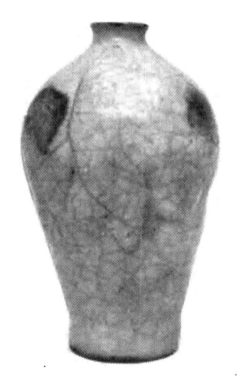

159

160

162

163

161   165

164

166

167

168

169

170

171

172

173

174 and 175

176 and 177

178

179

180

181

182

183

184

185

186

187

188

193

189

192

190

191

194

199

197

198

195

196

200

201

203

205

202

204

206

207

208

214

215

209, 210, and 211

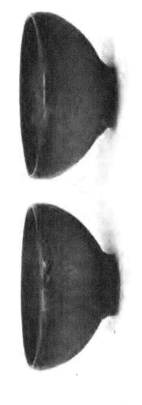

212 and 213

216

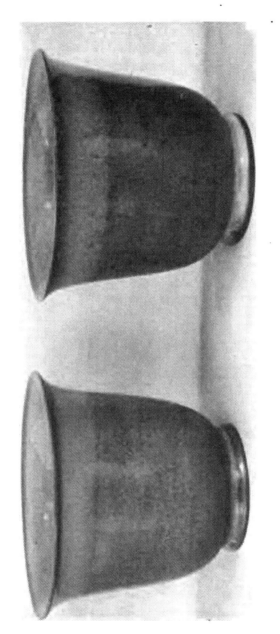

217 and 218

219

221

220

222

223

224

225

226

227

229

228

230

231

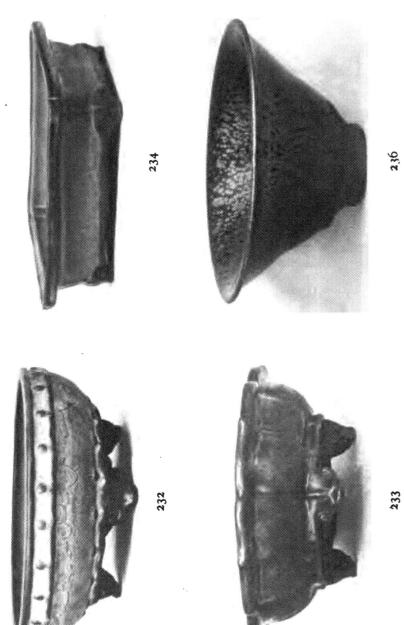

234

2,36

232

233

235

237

242

238

243

239

245

241

244

240

246

247

249

248

250

251

252

258

257

255

254

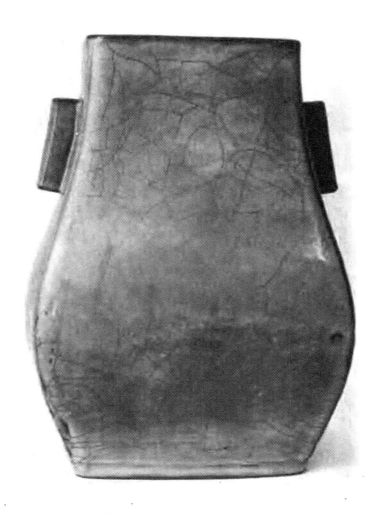

253

256

259

260

261

266

262   263

264   265

267   268

269   270 and 271

273

278

274

279

275

276 and 277

280

281   282

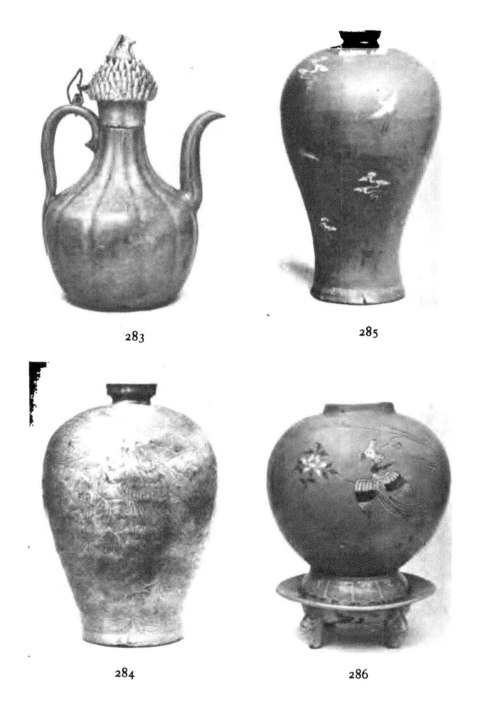

283

285

284

286

287

290

291

289

292

288

295

293

296

294

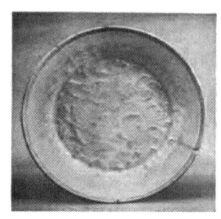

297

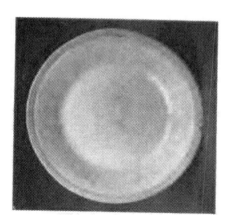

298

299

300

301

303

309

302

313

310

312

311

304

305

306 and 307

308

314

315, 316 and 319

320

317 and 318

321

322

323

324

325

326

327

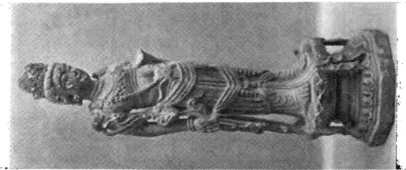

328

329

330

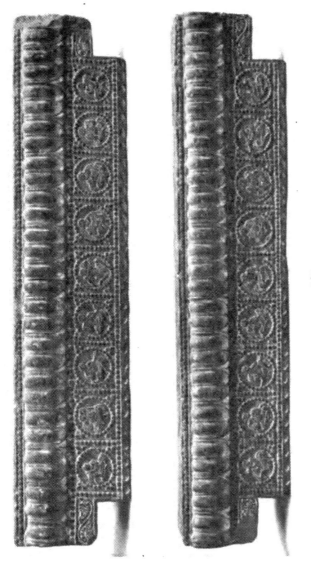

331

333

334

334 (detail)

335

336

337

338

339

340

341

342

343

CPSIA information can be obtained
at www.ICGtesting.com
Printed in the USA
BVHW050153190121
597730BV00020B/638